THE ULTIMATE VERMONT TRAVEL GUIDE 2023

Discover Vermont's Natural Beauty and Hidden Gems, Insider Tips and Itineraries for an Unforgettable 2023 Trip

Christopher Brownell

D1525650

All rights reserved.

TABLE OF CONTENT

CHAPTER 5

Vermont for Families

Family-friendly activities and attractions

Kid-friendly dining and accommodations

Tips for traveling with kids in Vermont

CHAPTER 6

Sustainable Vermont

Eco-friendly tourism in Vermont

Sustainable lodging and dining options

Local initiatives to protect Vermont's environment

CHAPTER 7

Practical Information

Essential travel tips

Safety advice

APPENDIX

CONCLUSION

INTRODUCTION

Vermont, the home of green mountains, maple syrup, and breathtaking landscapes, has long drawn people from all over the world. Vermont is more popular than ever in 2023, with visitors coming to the state to enjoy its distinct combination of natural beauty, small-town charm, and thriving cultural environment.

As you travel around Vermont, you'll immediately realize that each state has its distinct personality. Vermonters are noted for their self-reliance, love of the outdoors, and dedication to community and sustainability. It's a destination where you can stroll through gorgeous forests, ski down snow-covered slopes, sample artisanal cheeses and specialty brews, and meet friendly residents eager to share their tales and traditions. Whether you're a first-time visitor or a seasoned tourist, Vermont always has something fresh to offer. The state's beautiful countryside comes alive with wildflowers in the summer, and farmers' markets and festivals celebrate the abundance of the season. Autumn provides a riot of color as the leaves shift to colors of gold, crimson, and orange, and travelers come to the state to experience this spectacular display of natural beauty. In the winter, the snow-covered hills and valleys of Vermont transform into a paradise for skiers, snowboarders, and other winter sports lovers.

But Vermont is more than simply a destination for outdoor activities. The state also boasts a thriving cultural landscape, with world-class museums, galleries, and performing arts facilities showcasing the work of both local and national, and international artists and performers. Burlington, Vermont's biggest city, is a cultural hotspot, with a flourishing music scene, award-winning restaurants, and a lively waterfront that holds a variety of events throughout the year.

Vermont is the ideal destination for anyone wishing to relax and refresh. Little towns and villages in the state provide an opportunity to slow down and enjoy the basic joys of life, from a leisurely walk around the town center to a comfortable lunch by the fire at a local inn. Additionally, with a focus on sustainability and responsible tourism, Vermont is a location that enables tourists to meaningfully interact with nature and the community. When you travel around Vermont, you will discover that the state's natural beauty is unparalleled. Vermont's environment is stunning, from the rolling hills of the Champlain Valley to the rocky peaks of the Green Mountains. With over 70 state parks and forests, there are infinite chances to experience the great outdoors, whether hiking, bicycling, fishing, or just admiring the scenery.

Vermont is also well-known for its farm-to-table food and handcrafted goods. The rich countryside of the state generates a variety of fresh, locally produced fruits and vegetables, which can be obtained at farmers' markets and roadside stands around the state. Vermont is also a foodie's delight, with a thriving craft beer and cider sector, as well as award-winning cheeses and chocolates. Vermont's dedication to sustainability and responsible tourism is one of the factors that distinguish it from other locations. Vermonters care greatly about the environment and take pleasure in preserving the state's natural riches for future generations. Vermont is a leader in sustainability, from organic agricultural techniques to green energy programs, and tourists can feel good about supporting companies and organizations that are devoted to having a positive influence on the planet.

Vermont has plenty to offer everyone, from outdoor lovers to foodies to cultural seekers. Vermont should be on every traveler's bucket list because of its magnificent natural beauty, vibrant cultural scene, and devotion to sustainability. Therefore, why not plan a vacation to Vermont in 2023 to see all this beautiful state has to offer?

WELCOME TO VERMONT

Vermont is a country of lush mountains, scenic lakes, and attractive small villages. Vermont is a state in the northeastern United States known for its magnificent natural beauty, rich history, and distinct culture. Vermont is a small state, but it delivers a powerful punch in terms of natural beauty. The Green Mountains, which extend from north to south across the state, is a popular destination for hikers, cyclists, and skiers. Apart from the mountains, Vermont has approximately 800 lakes and ponds, including Lake

Champlain, the sixth biggest lake in the United States. Visitors are drawn to Vermont for its natural beauty, but it is also known for its beautiful small towns and villages. These towns are rich in old structures, charming shops, and friendly locals who are eager to share their tales and customs with tourists. Stowe, Woodstock, and Manchester are among Vermont's most popular towns.

Vermont's dedication to sustainability and responsible tourism is one of the factors that distinguish it from other states. Vermonters care greatly about the environment and take pleasure in preserving the state's natural riches for future generations. Vermont is a leader in sustainability, from organic agricultural techniques to green energy programs, and tourists can feel good about supporting companies and organizations that are devoted to having a positive influence on the planet. Vermont is also recognized for its distinct culture and rich history. Visitors may tour historic sites such as the Ethan Allen Homestead and the Bennington Battlefield, which played an important part in the American Revolution. Vermont also has a thriving arts culture, with world-class museums, galleries, and performing arts facilities showcasing the work of both local and national, and international artists and performers.

Vermont is a foodie's dream when it comes to cuisine. The state is well-known for its farm-to-table food and handcrafted goods. The rich countryside of the state generates a variety of fresh, locally produced fruits and vegetables, which can be obtained at farmers' markets and roadside stalls around the state. Vermont is also a culinary destination not to be missed, with a thriving craft beer and cider sector, as well as award-winning cheeses and chocolates.

Vermont has a lot to offer in terms of outdoor activities. Visitors may enjoy hiking, bicycling, fishing, and swimming in the state's lakes and ponds throughout the summer. The state's forests come alive with autumn colors in the fall, and travelers rush to the state to watch this breathtaking display of natural beauty. In the winter, the snow-covered hills and valleys of Vermont transform into a paradise for skiers, snowboarders, and other winter sports lovers. Vermont also has world-class ski destinations such as Stowe Mountain Resort, Killington Resort, and Okemo Mountain Resort. Skiing, snowboarding, cross-country skiing, and snowshoeing are among the winter sports available at these resorts. These resorts, with their warm lodges, gourmet cuisine, and spa services, are the perfect location to rest and relax after a day on the slopes.

Vermont is a vacation location that has something for everyone. Vermont is the ideal destination for outdoor adventures, cultural experiences, or just a place to rest and relax. Vermont should be on every traveler's bucket list because of its spectacular natural beauty, rich history, distinct culture, and devotion to sustainability. So why not schedule a vacation to Vermont now and see what this amazing state has to offer?

WHY VISIT VERMONT IN 2023?

Vermont is a lovely state in the northeastern United States that has a lot to offer tourists. There are several reasons to visit Vermont in 2023, from its spectacular natural beauty and attractive small towns to its rich history and distinct culture.

Natural Beauty

The natural beauty of Vermont is one of the top reasons to come in 2023. The Green Mountains are a popular hiking, biking, and skiing destination in the state. Moreover, Vermont has approximately 800 lakes and ponds, including Lake Champlain, the sixth-biggest lake in the United States. Vermont is also well-known for its spectacular autumn foliage, which attracts people from all over the world.

Outdoor Activities

Vermont is an outdoor enthusiast's dream. Visitors may enjoy hiking, bicycling, fishing, and swimming in the state's lakes and ponds throughout the summer. Vermont's snow-covered hills and valleys transform into a paradise for skiers, snowboarders, and other winter sports lovers throughout the winter. Vermont also has world-class ski destinations such as Stowe Mountain Resort, Killington Resort, and Okemo Mountain Resort.

Small Town Charm

Vermont is well-known for its picturesque little towns and villages. These towns are rich in old structures, charming shops, and friendly locals who are eager to share their tales and customs with tourists. Stowe, Woodstock, and Manchester are among Vermont's most popular towns.

Culinary Delights

Vermont is a foodie's dream. The state is well-known for its farm-to-table food and handcrafted goods. The rich countryside of the state generates a variety of fresh, locally produced fruits and vegetables, which can be obtained at farmers' markets and roadside stalls around the state. Vermont is also a culinary destination not to be missed, with a thriving artisan beer and cider sector, as well as award-winning cheeses and chocolates.

Rich History

Visitors may tour historic places such as the Ethan Allen Homestead and the Bennington Battlefield in Vermont, which played an important part in the American Revolution. Vermont also has various museums and historic sites that highlight the state's rich past, such as the Shelburne Museum and the Billings Farm & Museum.

Unique Culture

Vermont has a distinct culture that is deeply intertwined with its surroundings. Vermonters are devoted to sustainability and responsible tourism, and they take pleasure in safeguarding the state's natural resources for future generations. Vermont is a leader in sustainability, from organic agricultural techniques to green energy programs, and tourists can feel good about supporting companies and organizations that are devoted to having a positive influence on the planet. Vermont also has a thriving arts culture, with world-class museums, galleries, and performing arts facilities showcasing the work of both local and national, and international artists and performers.

Festivals and Special Events

During the year, Vermont hosts several festivals and events. There is always something going on in Vermont, from the Vermont Maple Festival in April to the Vermont Brewers Festival in July to the Stowe Foliage Arts Festival in October. These events are a terrific chance to learn about the state's culture and meet residents and other guests.

There are a variety of reasons to visit Vermont in 2023. Vermont offers something for everyone, whether you're seeking outdoor activities, small-town charm, culinary pleasures, rich history, distinct culture, or festivals and events. So why not schedule a vacation to Vermont now and see what this amazing state has to offer?

CHAPTER 1

PLANNING YOUR TRIP

Travel planning may be both thrilling and stressful, but with the appropriate knowledge, it can be a breeze. This area of the Vermont Travel Guide 2023 is intended to give useful information for planning your vacation to Vermont.

When to Visit Vermont

Vermont is a year-round destination, with each season having its distinct appeal. Summer (June to August) is the most popular season to come, with nice weather and an abundance of outdoor activities. The spectacular autumn foliage attracts people from all over the world throughout the fall season (September to November). Skiing, snowboarding, and other winter sports are available in the winter (December to February), while hiking and other outdoor activities are available in the spring (March to May).

How to Get to Vermont

Vermont may be reached by car, rail, bus, or air. Burlington International Airport and Rutland Southern Vermont Regional Airport are the largest airports in Vermont, with flights to major cities in the United States and Canada. Amtrak's Ethan Allen Express and Vermonter trains serve Vermont, as do Greyhound and Megabus, which provide bus service to key cities in the area.

What to Pack

Packing for Vermont is mostly determined by the season you want to travel. It is advisable to carry lightweight clothes, good walking shoes, sunscreen, and insect repellent throughout the summer months.

Bring warm clothes, such as coats, hats, and gloves, since the weather may turn rather cool in the autumn. Winter clothing, such as snow boots, gloves, and a thick coat, is required. Since spring is a transitional season, bring layers and wet gear.

Travel Documents & Visas

To enter the United States, international travelers must have a valid passport and a visa. Since the visa application procedure might take many weeks, it is critical to prepare ahead of time. Visitors may also need supplementary travel papers, such as an ESTA if they are coming from a Visa Waiver Program country. For the most up-to-date information on visa requirements and travel papers, visit the U.S. Department of State website.

Health and Safety Tips

Vermont is a safe place with low crime rates, although care should always be taken. It is strongly advised to obtain travel insurance to cover any unexpected medical costs. Even on cloudy days, visitors should keep hydrated and use sunscreen. Visitors should also be mindful of the risks of tick-borne infections, which are common throughout the state during the summer months.

Arranging a vacation in Vermont is a simple process with lots of tools to assist you along the way. You'll be well on your way to a successful and pleasurable journey to the Green Mountain State if you follow these recommendations and rules.

WHEN TO GO

Vermont is a year-round destination, with each season providing its own set of activities and attractions. Whether you're searching for outdoor experiences, cultural events, or just a chance to rest and unwind, there's a great time to visit Vermont for everyone.

Summer (June-August)

With mild weather and an abundance of outdoor activities, summer is the most popular season to visit Vermont. Hiking, bicycling, swimming, and boating are all popular activities for visitors, as are cultural events such as outdoor concerts and festivals. The state is recognized for its gorgeous lakes and rivers, and water-based sports including kayaking, paddle boarding, and fishing are popular.

The annual Vermont Brewers Festival, held in July in Burlington, is one of the most popular summer festivals in Vermont. Around 100 craft brewers from throughout the state and area will be present, as well as live music, food trucks, and other events.

Autumn (September-November)

The beautiful autumn foliage attracts travelers from all over the world, making October possibly the most attractive season to visit Vermont. The leaves turn color in late September and peak in mid-October, providing a breathtaking display of color over the state. Tourists may go apple picking, enjoy picturesque drives, and attend autumn festivals and fairs.

The Stowe Foliage Arts Festival, held in October in Stowe, is one of Vermont's most popular autumn festivals. Almost 150 artists and craftspeople will be on hand, as well as live music, food vendors, and other activities.

Winter (December-February)

Vermont in winter is a snowy paradise, with many options for skiing, snowboarding, snowshoeing, and other winter sports. The state is home to several ski resorts, including Killington, Stowe, and Jay Peak, which provide a variety of terrain and activities for skiers of all ability levels.

Sleigh rides, ice skating, and snowmobiling are all available to visitors. Throughout the winter, the state is also renowned for its comfortable inns and bed and breakfasts, which provide a warm and welcoming atmosphere.

Spring (March-May) (March-May)

In Vermont, spring is a transitional season, with the snow melting and the trees starting to blossom. This is an excellent time to come for hiking and other outdoor activities, as well as to take advantage of the state's maple syrup season. Visitors may visit local sugarhouses, learn about the maple syrup manufacturing process, and taste maple products such as syrup, candy, and cream.

The Vermont Maple Festival, held in April in St. Albans, is one of the most popular spring festivals in Vermont. There will be a procession, pancake breakfasts, maple syrup sampling, live music, and other events during the festival.

Vermont is a year-round vacation location. There's a great season to visit Vermont for everyone, whether you favor the warmth of summer, the beauty of autumn foliage, the excitement of winter sports, or the waking of spring.

HOW TO GET THERE

Traveling to Vermont is simple, whether by aircraft, car, bus, or train. Here's a breakdown of the most common modes of transportation to Vermont:

By Air

Burlington International Airport (BTV) is Vermont's busiest airport, with daily flights to and from New York, Boston, Chicago, and Washington, D.C. Delta, United, American, and JetBlue are among the airlines that fly to BTV. Rutland Southern Vermont Regional Airport and Lebanon Municipal Airport are two of the state's smaller regional airports.

By Car

By Car I-89, which runs north-south across the state, and I-91, which extends from the Canadian border to the Massachusetts border, are the primary roadways. Tourists may also travel beautiful roads through the state's lovely little villages and mountains, such as the Route 100 Byway.

By Bus

Greyhound and Megabus both serve Vermont, with daily trips to and from major locations including New York, Boston, and Montreal. Vermont Translines is a regional bus service that links municipalities throughout the state.

By Train

Amtrak's Vermonter train runs from Washington D.C. to St. Albans, Vermont, with stops in major cities such as New York, Philadelphia, and Boston. Smaller communities like as Brattleboro and White River Junction are also served by the train.

How to Get Around

There are various methods to move about and discover Vermont after you arrive:

By Car

Hiring a car is an excellent way to see Vermont since many of the state's attractions are spread and need a car to reach. Hertz, Avis, and Enterprise are among the main car rental firms in Vermont.

Taking Public Transportation

Vermont has a limited public transit system, however, there are various alternatives to driving. Local bus services are available in various communities, and Amtrak's Vermonter train makes stops across the state.

Using a Bicycle

Vermont is an excellent riding destination, with several gorgeous bike routes around the state. Visitors may explore the state's small towns and countryside by renting bicycles from local stores or bringing their own.

On Foot

Vermont is well-known for its hiking paths, which cater to hikers of all ability levels. Hiking paths in the state's mountains and forests range from small nature walks to multi-day backpacking treks.

Traveling to and around Vermont is straightforward and accessible. There are various ways to explore the state and see all it has to offer, whether you choose to travel by aircraft, vehicle, bus, rail, bicycle, or foot.

WHERE TO STAY

Vermont has a broad range of lodging alternatives for travelers, from small bed & breakfasts to luxurious resorts. These are some of the greatest Vermont lodging options:

Bed & Breakfast

Vermont is well-known for its attractive bed and breakfasts, many of which are housed in historic houses and structures. These intimate hotels provide a warm atmosphere and customized service, which often includes prepared breakfasts and afternoon snacks. The Rabbit Hill Inn in Lower Waterford, the Inn at Weston in Weston, and the Swift House Inn in Middlebury are all popular Vermont bed and breakfasts.

Resorts and Hotels

Vermont has several hotels and resorts that provide exquisite lodgings and services. Several of these homes are in picturesque places, such as the Green Mountains or Lake Champlain, and include outdoor activities such as skiing, golfing, and hiking. The Stowe Mountain Lodge in Stowe, the Essex Resort and Spa in Essex Junction, and the Basin Harbor Club in Vergennes are all popular Vermont hotels and resorts.

Cottages and Cabins

Visitors looking for a more rural experience may rent cabins or cottages in Vermont's countryside. Our comfortable lodgings allow you to detach from the outer world and enjoy the peaceful surroundings.

Several cabins and cottages include complete kitchens and outside barbecues, enabling guests to prepare their meals. The Vermont Country Cottage in Weston, the Woodstock Hotel and Resort Cottages in Woodstock, and the Lake Morey Resort Cottages in Fairlee are all popular cabin and cottage rentals in Vermont.

Campgrounds

Vermont's natural beauty makes it an ideal camping destination, with various campsites located around the state. Campgrounds range from simple tent sites to RV parks with full hookups, and many include amenities like showers, laundry facilities, and playgrounds. Green Mountain Family Campground in Bristol, Smugglers' Notch State Park Campsite in Stowe, and the Quechee Pine Valley KOA in Quechee are all popular Vermont campgrounds.

Vacation Rentals

Vacation rentals are an excellent choice for individuals seeking extra room and privacy. Vermont has a broad range of vacation rentals available, including apartments, condos, and houses. These homes are often completely furnished with kitchens, washing facilities, and other amenities, making them ideal for families or groups of friends. Vermont Vacation Rentals in Killington, the Slopeside Okemo Condo in Ludlow, and the White Birch Cottage in Manchester are all popular vacation rentals in Vermont.

Vermont has a variety of lodging alternatives to accommodate every traveler's requirements and interests. Vermont provides something for everyone, whether you want a comfortable bed & breakfast, a magnificent resort, a rustic cottage, or a huge vacation rental.

WHAT TO PACK

Because of the state's ever-changing weather patterns, packing for a vacation to Vermont might be challenging. Here are some packing suggestions for a vacation to Vermont:

Clothing

Since the weather in Vermont may change fast, it's vital to prepare clothes for all seasons. Summers in Vermont are often warm, with highs in the 70s and 80s Fahrenheit (21-27 Celsius). Bring summer shorts, T-shirts, and lightweight slacks, as well as a light jacket or sweater for cold nights.

Autumn is one of the most popular seasons for tourists in Vermont, with spectacular leaf displays all around the state. Throughout the day, temperatures might vary from the 30s to the 60s Fahrenheit (0-15 Celsius), so dress in layers. A light jacket or sweater, a rain jacket, and appropriate hiking or walking shoes are required.

Winter in Vermont may be very cold and snowy, with temperatures often falling below freezing. Warm gear, such as thick jackets, boots, hats, gloves, and scarves, should be packed. Layering is essential for keeping warm, so bring thermal underwear, long-sleeved shirts, and sweaters.

With temps ranging from the 30s to the 60s Fahrenheit, spring in Vermont may be unpredictable (0-15 Celsius). Bring layers, such as a rain jacket or umbrella, as well as appropriate walking or hiking shoes.

Footwear

Comfortable shoes are essential for any vacation to Vermont, particularly if you want to do any hiking or other outdoor activities. Bring a strong pair of hiking boots or trail shoes, as well as a pair of comfortable walking shoes or sneakers. Pack waterproof footwear with a strong grip for navigating snow and ice in the winter.

Accessories

Vermont's weather may be unpredictable, so bring a few things to keep you comfortable. Winter vacations need a warm hat, gloves, and scarf, whilst summer visits require a sun hat and sunglasses. A rain jacket or umbrella is also recommended since Vermont is notorious for frequent rain showers.

Outdoor Gear

If you want to participate in any outside activities, such as hiking or skiing, you need to bring adequate equipment. On hiking trips, bring a backpack with water, food, and extra clothing, as well as a map or GPS device. In the winter, bring ski or snowboard equipment or rent it from one of Vermont's numerous ski resorts.

Miscellaneous Items

Apart from clothes and outdoor gear, there are a few more essentials to bring for a vacation to Vermont. Bring a reusable water bottle with you since Vermont's tap water is safe to drink and there are several public water fountains across the state. Don't forget to bring your camera to record the breathtaking views, as well as a book or travel guide to help you organize your schedule.

Preparing for a vacation to Vermont takes some thought and planning, but with the correct clothes, footwear, and accessories, you may be comfortable and prepared for all weather conditions.

CHAPTER 2

DISCOVERING VERMONT

Vermont is a small state in the northeastern United States recognized for its natural beauty, pleasant communities, and possibilities for outdoor leisure. Vermont has a lot to offer, from the spectacular autumn foliage to world-class skiing and snowboarding. These are some of the highlights of what you may find in Vermont.

Outdoor Activities

Vermont is a paradise for outdoor lovers, with many chances for hiking, bicycling, skiing, snowboarding, and other activities. The Green Mountains, which stretch the length of the state, are home to miles of hiking routes, including the well-known Long Trail and the Appalachian Trail. Vermont also has various ski resorts, such as Stowe Mountain Resort, Killington

Resort, and Sugarbush Resort, which provide some of the greatest skiing and snowboarding in the nation.

Vermont is also an excellent destination for fishing, hunting, kayaking, and canoeing. There are around 800 lakes and ponds in the state, as well as several rivers and streams. Fishermen may try their luck capturing trout, bass, and other species, while hunters can explore the state's vast public lands.

Food and Beverage

Vermont is well-known for its farm-to-table cuisine and artisanal food and wine. Several small family farms in the state produce cheese, maple syrup, and other items using traditional techniques. Guests may go on a maple syrup farm tour, enjoy handmade cheese, and try local craft beer and cider.

Burlington, Vermont's biggest city, is an excellent starting point for exploring the state's food and beverage industry. Magic Hat Brewing Company and Switchback Brewing Company are two of the city's microbreweries. Tourists may also visit the Burlington Farmers' Market, which sells locally-grown food, baked goods, and handcrafted crafts.

Culture and History

Vermont has a long history that dates back to its first Native American settlers. Tourists may learn about the state's history by visiting its numerous museums and historic places, such as the Shelburne Museum, which has 39 structures on 45 acres of land, and the Ethan Allen Homestead, which was the home of the famous Revolutionary War hero Ethan Allen.

Vermont also has a vibrant arts and cultural scene. The state is well-known for its performing arts facilities, including Burlington's Flynn Center for the Performing Arts, as well as its many art galleries and festivals. Montpelier, the state capital, has various museums and galleries, including the T.W. Wood Gallery and the Vermont History Museum.

Natural Beauty

Vermont's natural beauty is perhaps its most appealing feature. Visitors come from all over the world to see the state's rolling hills, deep forests, and pristine lakes and rivers. Vermont's mountains come alive with a magnificent display of leaves in the autumn, drawing leaf-peepers from all around. Many national and state parks may also be found in Vermont, including the Green Mountain National Forest and Lake Champlain Islands State Park.

Vermont also has several attractive small towns and villages, each with its distinct personality. Stowe, for example, is recognized for its gorgeous Main Street, which is lined with charming shops and restaurants, and Woodstock is known for its historic covered bridges.

Vermont is a discovery-filled state, from its natural beauty to its rich history and culture. Vermont has something for everyone, whether you're an outdoor enthusiast, a foodie, or a history lover.

THE BEST SCENIC DRIVES

A picturesque drive is one of the greatest ways to appreciate Vermont's natural beauty. The state's winding roads provide breathtaking views of mountains, forests, and lakes and are an excellent way to explore the area at leisure. These are some of Vermont's most picturesque highways.

Route 100

Route 100, which runs the length of Vermont from north to south, is one of the most picturesque routes in the state. The route passes through attractive small towns and rolling hills, providing breathtaking views of the Green Mountains. Visitors may stop along the road at historic covered bridges, local farms, and small rural boutiques.

The Lake Champlain Islands

The Lake Champlain Islands, situated in Vermont's northwest region, provide some of the most magnificent views in the state. Tourists may enjoy a picturesque drive along Route 2, which follows along the lake's shores and provides views of the far

Adirondack Mountains. Many state parks, including Burton Island State Park and Grand Isle State Park, are located on the islands and feature hiking trails, swimming, and boating.

The Mad River Byway

The Mad River Byway runs through Warren, Waitsfield, and Moretown in central Vermont, following the Mad River. The route provides breathtaking views of the Mad River Valley, as well as the Green Mountains in the distance. Visitors may stop at various local businesses along the path, including craft brewers and artisanal food makers.

The Northeast Kingdom

The Northeast Kingdom is a sparsely populated area in northeastern Vermont recognized for its rugged beauty. Route 114, which passes through lush forests and various lakes and rivers, is a lovely journey for visitors. Many state parks, including Lake Willoughby State Park and Brighton State Park, are located in the area and provide hiking trails, fishing, and camping.

The Route 7 Corridor

The Route 7 Corridor stretches from Bennington in the south to Burlington in the north of Vermont. The route provides spectacular views of the Green Mountains as well as various historic buildings and beautiful small villages. Visitors may stop along the journey at the Bennington Battle Monument, the Shelburne Museum, and the lovely village of Manchester.

The Appalachian Gap

The Appalachian Gap, situated in the middle of the Green Mountains, is a difficult journey that rewards some of the state's most breathtaking views. Route 17 winds its way up and over the mountain pass, providing panoramic views of the surrounding peaks. Visitors may stop at the Appalachian Gap Overlook at the top of the gap for breathtaking views of the Champlain Valley.

Vermont has several beautiful routes, each with its distinct perspective of the state's natural beauty. Whether you're searching for charming small villages, rugged mountain landscapes, or stunning lakes and rivers, Vermont has a scenic journey for you.

OUTDOOR ACTIVITIES FOR ALL SEASONS

Vermont is an outdoor enthusiast's dream, with a wide range of activities available all year. Vermont has something for everyone, from skiing and snowboarding in the winter to hiking and fishing in the summer.

These are some of Vermont's top outdoor activities for all seasons.

Winter Activities:

Snowboarding and skiing

Vermont has some of the country's best ski resorts, including Stowe Mountain Resort, Killington Resort, and Sugarbush Resort. These resorts provide a wide range of trails for skiers of all abilities, as well as amenities such as ski schools, rental equipment, and après-ski activities.

Snowshoeing

Snowshoeing is a more peaceful winter activity. Vermont's many state parks and nature preserves have snowshoeing trails, allowing visitors to explore the state's forests and mountains at their leisure.

Ice Skating

Ice Skating The outdoor rink at Burlington Waterfront Park and the indoor rink at the Gutterson Fieldhouse in Burlington are both popular.

Spring Activities:

Maple Sugar

Vermont's maple trees begin to produce sap in the early spring, which is then turned into maple syrup. Several sugarhouses around Vermont provide tours and demonstrations of the maple sugaring process, allowing visitors to learn about this famous Vermont institution.

Hiking

Hiking The Long Trail, the Appalachian Trail, and Camel's Hump are all popular spring walks.

Fishing

Spring is also an excellent season for fishing in Vermont's many lakes and rivers. Trout, bass, and walleye are among the many fish species found in the state.

Summer Activities:

Swimming

Vermont has several gorgeous lakes and rivers, making it an ideal swimming vacation. Lake Champlain, Silver Lake State Park, and the Quechee Gorge are among the most popular swimming places.

Biking

Vermont's picturesque roads and trails make it an ideal bike destination. The state's beautiful little towns and gorgeous scenery may be explored on two wheels, with possibilities ranging from easy rides to tough mountain biking tracks.

Kayaking and canoeing

Canoeing and kayaking are other popular activities on Vermont's numerous lakes and rivers. Guests may hire or bring their boats to explore the state's waterways at their leisure.

Autumn Activities:

Leaf Peeping

Fall is a popular time to visit Vermont for its stunning foliage. To experience the state's spectacular autumn colors, visitors may take beautiful drives, climb through the mountains, or even take a hot air balloon flight.

Apple Picking

The fall season is also ideal for apple picking in Vermont's many orchards. Visitors can take in the crisp autumn air while picking their apples, followed by fresh apple cider and cider donuts.

Hunting

Hunting Season in Vermont begins in the fall, with chances to hunt deer, moose, and other game animals. Visitors can go on guided hunting trips or simply enjoy the many nature preserves and wildlife refuges in the state.

Vermont has a broad range of outdoor activities throughout the year, making it an ideal location for nature lovers and outdoor enthusiasts. Vermont has something for everyone, whether you're seeking for adrenaline-pumping winter sports or relaxing summer pastimes.

MUSEUMS AND HISTORICAL SITES

Vermont has a rich history, dating back to its early colonial days and continuing through its participation in the American Revolution and beyond. Visitors to Vermont may learn about the state's rich history by visiting one of its numerous historic sites and museums. These are some of the best historic places and museums in Vermont to visit.

Shelburne Museum

The Shelburne Museum, in Shelburne, Vermont, is a one-of-a-kind museum that exhibits American art and design as well as Vermont history. Over 45 acres, the museum includes 39 structures, including old cottages, farms, and a lighthouse. Visitors can look through exhibits ranging from quilts and textiles to folk art and furniture.

Ethan Allen Homestead Museum

Ethan Allen was a founding father of Vermont and a hero of the American Revolution. His homestead has been preserved as a museum dedicated to his life and legacy in Burlington, Vermont. Visitors can take a tour of Allen's historic home and learn about his role in Vermont's history.

Bennington Battle Monument

The Bennington Battle Monument is a 306-foot-tall obelisk in Bennington, Vermont, commemorating the Battle of Bennington, a pivotal battle in the American Revolution. Visitors can take an elevator to the top of the monument to get a bird's-eye view of the surrounding countryside.

Vermont State House

The Vermont State House is the state capital building and a fine example of Greek Revival architecture in Montpelier, Vermont. Visitors may take a tour of the facility and learn about the legislative process in Vermont.

Hildene, The Lincoln Family Home

Hildene, near Manchester, Vermont, was the vacation residence of President Abraham Lincoln's son, Robert

Todd Lincoln. The historic home has been maintained as a museum, providing visitors with an insight into the lives of one of America's most famous families.

Calvin Coolidge Homestead District

The Calvin Coolidge Homestead District, situated in Plymouth, Vermont, is President Calvin Coolidge's birthplace and boyhood home. Guests may take a tour of Coolidge's historic house and learn about his life and administration.

Rokeby Museum

The Rokeby Museum is a historic farm and museum in Ferrisburgh, Vermont, that chronicles the story of the Robinson family, who were Quaker abolitionists and social justice activists. Visitors to the historic home may take a tour and learn about the family's involvement in the Underground Railroad and other social justice initiatives.

Vermont Historical Society Museum

The Vermont Historical Society Museum in Montpelier, Vermont, provides an in-depth study into Vermont's history, from its early colonial days to the present. The museum's displays include topics ranging from agriculture and industry to Vermont's participation in the Civil War.

Justin Morrill Homestead

The Justin Morrill Homestead in Strafford, Vermont, was the residence of Justin Morrill, a United States Senator who was instrumental in the establishment of land-grant institutions in the United States. Guests may take a tour of Morrill's historic house and learn about his legacy.

American Precision Museum

In Windsor, Vermont, the American Precision Museum celebrates the history of precise manufacturing in the United States. The museum has displays ranging from weapons to clock manufacture, as well as hands-on activities for visitors of all ages.

Vermont's historic sites and museums provide tourists with a rich and intriguing glimpse into the state's history. Whether you're interested in the American Revolution, Vermont's agricultural past or the state's participation in the Civil War, Vermont's historic sites and museums provide something for everyone to explore and discover.

QUIRKY SMALL TOWNS TO EXPLORE

Vermont is known for its attractive small towns, each with its distinct personality and charm. Although many people come to the state's bigger cities, such as Burlington and Montpelier, there are many small villages worth seeing as well. These are five of Vermont's most unique tiny towns to visit.

Woodstock

Woodstock, Vermont, is a classic New England village with tree-lined streets, lovely shops, and historic residences. Tourists may visit the town's various art galleries and antique stores, as well as the Billings Farm & Museum, which provides an insight into Vermont's agricultural history.

Stowe

Stowe, situated in northern Vermont, is a renowned ski town with lots to do in the summer. Tourists may stroll around the town's various shops and eateries or enjoy a picturesque drive down Smugglers' Notch. The Trapp Family Lodge, which inspired "The Sound of Music," is also located in Stowe.

Manchester

Manchester, Vermont, is a shopper's dream, with hundreds of outlet stores and boutique shops. Tourists may also visit the town's numerous historic attractions, including the old vacation home of Robert Todd Lincoln, the Hildene estate.

Brattleboro

Brattleboro, Vermont's southernmost town, is a bohemian haven with a strong cultural scene. Tourists may stroll around the town's numerous galleries and art studios, or visit the Brattleboro Farmer's Market, which sells local vegetables and crafts.

Waitsfield

Waitsfield is a small community in central Vermont with a huge personality. Tourists may stroll around the town's shops and eateries or enjoy a picturesque drive across the Mad River Valley. Waitsfield is also home to Mad River Distillers, which provides tours and samples of its locally distilled beverages.

Grafton

Grafton is a historic town in southern Vermont with a picturesque main street lined with stores and eateries. The Grafton Village Cheese Company, which gives tours and tastes of their famous cheddar cheese, is one of the town's numerous historic landmarks.

Middlebury

Middlebury, Vermont's primary college town, has a flourishing arts and entertainment scene. Tourists may wander through the Middlebury Farmers' Market, which sells local vegetables and crafts, or visit the town's various galleries and museums.

Randolph

Randolph Randolph is a small town in central Vermont with a huge heart. Tourists may visit the town's various historic attractions, such as the Chandler Music Hall, which hosts concerts and other cultural events all year.

Wilmington

Wilmington, in southern Vermont, is a charming town with a lively main street. Tourists may stroll around the town's shops and eateries or enjoy a picturesque drive along the neighboring Molly Stark Byway.

Chester

Chester, in southern Vermont, is a lovely town with a fascinating history. Tourists may visit the town's various historic attractions, such as the Chester Station, which was formerly a significant train stop.

Vermont's small villages allow tourists to experience the state's distinct charm and character. There is something for everyone in Vermont's eccentric tiny towns, whether you're searching for outdoor experiences, shopping, and cuisine, or a peek into Vermont's rich past.

FARMERS' MARKETS AND FOODIE DESTINATIONS

The quantity of fresh, locally farmed food is one of the delights of visiting Vermont. From farm-to-table restaurants to farmers' markets, the state provides plenty of opportunities for foodies to sample Vermont's delicacies.

Farmers' Markets

Vermont has a rich agricultural heritage, and farmers' markets have long been a part of the state's food landscape. Farmers' markets may be found in towns and cities around the state from May to October. These markets provide an opportunity to purchase fresh, locally produced vegetables, as well as artisanal cheeses, baked products, and other specialty foods.

The Burlington Farmers' Market, which takes place every Saturday from May through October in downtown Burlington, is one of Vermont's most popular farmers' markets. Almost 90 sellers offer everything from fresh vegetables to cooked cuisine and crafts at the market. The Montpelier Farmer's Market, the Stowe Farmers' Market, and the Brattleboro Farmers' Market are all popular.

Foodie Destinations

Vermont also has several culinary hotspots. These places allow you to sample the finest of Vermont cuisine, from farm-to-table eateries to artisanal food producers.

Waterbury is one of Vermont's most popular foodie destinations. Waterbury, Vermont, is home to numerous well-known food and beverage manufacturers, including Ben & Jerry's Ice Cream, the Cool Hollow Cider Mill, and the Cabot Creamery Annex. Visitors may visit these factories and sample the delectable items they manufacture.

Another renowned foodie visit is the town of Shelburne, situated immediately south of Burlington. Shelburne is home to the 1,400-acre Shelburne Farms, a national historic site. The farm has a farm-to-table restaurant and a cheese-making facility, as well as tours and educational events.

Manchester, Vermont is another famous foodie destination. Manchester, Vermont, is home to various high-end restaurants and specialized food shops, as well as the well-known Equinox Resort & Spa. Guests may also explore the Hildene estate, Robert Todd

Lincoln's old vacation home, and sample the estate's award-winning wines.

Burlington is a foodie attraction in and of itself, with dozens of restaurants and specialized food outlets serving you a taste of Vermont cuisine. Burlington offers something for every foodie, from farm-to-table eateries like Hen of the Wood to specialized food shops like City Market.

Vermont's farmers' markets and foodie hotspots provide opportunities to sample the finest of Vermont cuisine, from fresh, locally produced vegetables to artisanal cheeses and other specialty foods. Whether you're a foodie searching for a culinary adventure or just want to sample the tastes of Vermont, the state's dynamic food industry has something for everyone.

CHAPTER 3

EXPLORING BURLINGTON

Burlington, Vermont's biggest city, is a popular tourist and local attraction. Burlington, situated along the shores of Lake Champlain, provides a unique combination of natural beauty and urban amenities. Burlington offers something for everyone, whether you like outdoor activities, shopping, or cultural attractions.

Outdoor Activities

Burlington's close to Lake Champlain and the neighboring mountains is one of its main attractions. Hiking, bicycling, boating, and fishing are just a few of the activities available to outdoor enthusiasts in the region. The Burlington Bike Path goes along the lakefront and provides stunning views of the water and the Adirondack Mountains across the lake. Waterfront Park, situated near the bike path's southern end, is a popular location for picnics, concerts, and other activities.

Burlington is a popular skiing and snowboarding destination in the winter. The surrounding Stowe and Jay Peak mountains provide world-class skiing and snowboarding, and the Bolton Valley Ski Resort is only a short drive from downtown Burlington. In Lake Champlain, ice skating and ice fishing are other popular winter pastimes.

Dining and Shopping

Burlington is also a shopping and dining destination. Almost 100 stores and restaurants may be found in the Church Street Marketplace, a pedestrian-only shopping and dining neighborhood. The street is lined with ancient buildings and has a bustling atmosphere both during the day and at night. There are local shops, artisanal food stores, and national chain businesses in the region.

Foodies will like Burlington's culinary culture as well. Burlington has something for everyone's taste, from farm-to-table restaurants to craft brewers. The Farmhouse Tap and Grill, which provides locally produced food and beverages, and the Skinny Pancake, which specializes in crepes prepared from local products, are two popular dining options.

Cultural Attractions

Burlington also has several cultural attractions. The Flynn Center for the Performing Arts is a historic theater that holds events ranging from Broadway plays to concerts by world-class performers. The Fleming Museum of Art at the University of Vermont has collections of art and artifacts from all over the world, while the ECHO Leahy Center for Lake Champlain is a science museum dedicated to the ecology and history of Lake Champlain.

The Shelburne Museum, a collection of historic buildings and artifacts, and the Ethan Allen Homestead Museum, which tells the tale of one of Vermont's most famous citizens, are two other cultural attractions. The Church Street Marketplace also hosts several street performers and artists, contributing to the city's thriving cultural environment.

Burlington is a must-see attraction for anybody traveling to Vermont. This vibrant city on the beaches of Lake Champlain has something for everyone with its mix of outdoor activities, shopping, eating, and cultural attractions.

THE QUEEN CITY'S TOP ATTRACTIONS

Burlington, Vermont, sometimes known as Queen City, is a pleasant and dynamic city with a lot to offer tourists. Burlington offers something for everyone, from historic sites to cultural attractions. Following are some of the city's main attractions:

Church Street Market

The Church Street Marketplace, situated in the center of Burlington, is a pedestrian-only shopping and dining area. It has about 100 stores, restaurants, and cafés in old structures. Tourists may take a walk along the cobblestone streets and shop at small shops, artisanal food stores, and national chain stores.

Lake Champlain

Lake Champlain is a breathtaking natural wonder that surrounds Burlington. Boating, fishing, and kayaking are all popular water sports on the lake. Around the lake, there are various beaches where people may swim and sunbathe. Visitors may also enjoy ice skating, ice fishing, and cross-country skiing on the lake in the winter.

Shelburne Museum

The Shelburne Museum is a one-of-a-kind and intriguing site situated south of Burlington. The museum has nearly 150,000 pieces, including historic structures, artwork, and artifacts. A 19th-century lighthouse, a riverboat, a covered bridge, and a variety of other structures that have been transferred to the museum's 45-acre complex are available for visitors to explore.

Ethan Allen Homestead Museum

The Ethan Allen Homestead Museum is a historic landmark in Burlington, Vermont, situated on the banks of the Winooski River. The museum honors the life and legacy of Ethan Allen, an American Revolutionary War hero and one of Vermont's most famous residents. Guests may take a tour of the reconstructed 18th-century farmhouse and learn about Allen's role in the establishment of Vermont.

Flynn Center for the Performing Arts

The Flynn Center for the Performing Arts is a historic theater in Burlington, Vermont. During the year, the theater presents a variety of events, including Broadway productions, concerts, dance performances, and comedy acts. The Flynn Center is a cultural center in Burlington that everyone interested in the performing arts should visit.

ECHO Leahy Center for Lake Champlain

The ECHO Leahy Center for Lake Champlain is a scientific museum that covers Lake Champlain's ecology and history. For visitors of all ages, the museum offers interactive exhibitions, live animal shows, and hands-on activities. The museum also has a 3D cinema where educational films about the lake and its environment are shown.

University of Vermont's Fleming Museum of Art

The Fleming Museum of Art at the University of Vermont is a world-class museum with collections of art and artifacts from all around the world. The museum's collection contains ancient Egyptian, Greek, and Roman works of art, as well as modern art and artifacts from Asia, Africa, and the Americas. During the year, rotating exhibits enhance the museum's permanent collection.

Vermont Teddy Bear Company

The Vermont Teddy Bear Company has been creating handcrafted teddy bears since 1981 and is a famous Vermont tradition. Guests may enjoy a guided tour of the factory and witness how the bears are manufactured. Visitors may also buy their own Vermont Teddy Bear from the company's on-site retail store.

Ben & Jerry's Factory

The Ben & Jerry's Factory is situated in Waterbury, Vermont, only a short drive from Burlington. Visitors to the plant may take a guided tour and observe how the famous ice cream is prepared. The tour includes a stop at the Flavor Graveyard, where retiring flavors are honored, as well as a sample of the highlighted flavor of the day.

BEST PLACES TO EAT AND DRINK

Burlington, like the rest of Vermont, is known for its farm-to-table food and craft drinks. The Queen City has several restaurants and bars that highlight the state's locally produced foods and unique culinary creations.

Hen of the Wood, located in the historic Hotel Vermont, is one of the most popular locations in town. Dishes like Vermont rabbit pappardelle and Vermont pork chop with apple mustard show the restaurant's emphasis on local foods. In addition to an exceptional wine selection, Hen of the Wood includes a comfortable bar area with specialty drinks.

Farmhouse Tap & Grill, which offers traditional American food with a Vermont twist, is another must-visit. The Farm Burger with Cabot cheddar and maple aioli and the maple glazed pork belly with grilled peaches are among the menu items. Farmhouse also offers a large beer selection, with over 25 beers on tap from Vermont and other states.

Leunig's Bistro & Café offers a more sophisticated eating experience. This French-inspired restaurant on Church Street has a lovely outside terrace with views of Lake Champlain. Escargots in puff pastry and roasted rack of lamb with black olive tapenade are among the delicacies on the menu. Leunig's also boasts a large wine list and a selection of cocktails.

In terms of beverages, Burlington boasts a booming craft beer culture. Zero Gravity Craft Brewery, which has two sites in Burlington, is one of the most popular brewers in town. The Pine Street brewery and taproom serve wood-fired pizzas and other small meals, as well as a changing range of beers on tap. The North End version of the brewery is a bigger area with a complete menu of beer, cider, and wine.

Foam Brewers, situated on the riverfront in Burlington's South End, is another must-see for beer lovers. Foam's industrial-chic facility has views of Lake Champlain and the Adirondack Mountains, as well as a changing selection of creative beers on tap. The brewery also has a small kitchen where refreshments such as charcuterie platters and soft pretzels are served.

If you're looking for a good drink, go to The Daily Planet. This trendy restaurant and bar has been a Burlington institution for over 30 years and offers a changing menu of creative drinks. The Daily Planet also features a large wine list and a selection of small meals.

Honey Road is a one-of-a-kind eating experience. This Middle Eastern restaurant on Church Street features meals such as falafel, lamb kofta, and spanakopita. Honey Road also features an amazing wine selection and a range of creative drinks.

Lake Champlain Chocolates is a must-see on any vacation to Burlington. This neighborhood chocolatier has been manufacturing handmade chocolates since 1983 and offers a wide range of delectable delicacies.

The firm also provides factory tours and a chocolate-making workshop.

Burlington boasts a vibrant food and beverage industry that highlights Vermont's locally produced foods and inventive culinary creations. The Queen City has something for everyone, whether you're looking for farm-to-table food or artisan beer.

FESTIVALS AND CULTURAL EVENTS

Vermont has a vibrant cultural environment, with festivals and events held throughout the year to highlight everything from music and art to cuisine and agriculture. If you're planning a vacation to Vermont, don't miss out on some of the best cultural events and festivals.

Burlington Discover Jazz Festival

The Burlington Discover Jazz Festival is a 10-day jazz music event held in early June each year in Burlington. The festival includes jazz concerts by local and national performers, as well as jazz workshops, seminars, and screenings of films.

Stowe Arts Festival

The Stowe Arts Festival is a three-day festival held in the lovely village of Stowe every August. Almost 200 artists and craftspeople will be displaying their work at the event, which will also include live music, food vendors, and children's activities.

Vermont Cheesemakers Festival

The Vermont Cheesemakers Festival honors the state's booming artisanal cheese industry. The event is hosted at Shelburne Farms in July and features over 40 cheesemakers showcasing their cheeses, as well as local food vendors and live music.

Vermont Brewers Festival

The Vermont Brewers Festival is a two-day festival hosted on the Burlington waterfront in July. The event showcases over 100 Vermont and other specialty beers, as well as live music and food vendors.

Vermont Maple Festival

The Vermont Maple Festival takes place over three days and celebrates Vermont's famous maple syrup industry. The event, which takes place in St. Albans every April, includes maple syrup tastings, maple-themed food vendors, live music, and a parade.

Brattleboro Literary Festival

The Brattleboro Literary Festival is an annual event held in the town of Brattleboro in October. Readings and conversations by local and national writers, as well as writing workshops and children's programs, are all part of the festival.

Middlebury New Filmmakers Festival

The Middlebury New Filmmakers Festival is a four-day event held in August in Middlebury, Vermont. The festival features panel talks and Q&A sessions with filmmakers from across the world, as well as young and upcoming filmmakers from around the world.

Vermont History Expo

The Vermont History Expo is a two-day event hosted at the Tunbridge Fairgrounds every two years in June. The expo includes live music, food vendors, and children's activities, as well as displays and demonstrations on Vermont's rich history.

Vermont Quilt Festival

The Vermont Quilt Festival is a three-day event held in Essex Junction, Vermont, each June. Around 100 quilt exhibitions are on display, as well as quilt-making demonstrations, talks, and workshops.

Vermont Sheep & Wool Festival

The Vermont Sheep & Wool Festival is a two-day event held at the Tunbridge Fairgrounds in October. The event includes sheep and wool exhibitions, as well as spinning, weaving, and other fiber arts demonstrations.

During the year, Vermont hosts several smaller events and performances, such as live music, theater shows, and art exhibits. There's something for everyone in Vermont's diverse cultural landscape, whether you're a history buff, a foodie, or an art enthusiast.

OUTDOOR RECREATION NEAR THE CITY

Burlington, Vermont, is a thriving city on Lake Champlain's shores, surrounded by mountains and rolling hills. It's no wonder that with so much natural beauty, outdoor activity is a popular pastime in and around the city. There's something for everyone, from hiking and biking to water activities and skiing.

Cycling is one of the most popular outdoor activities in Burlington. The city is well-known for its bike-friendly streets and trails, and there are various rental choices available for guests who do not bring their cycles. The

Burlington Bike Path is a 7.5-mile track that travels along Lake Champlain's waterfront, providing breathtaking views of the lake and the Adirondack Mountains. Since the trail is flat and paved, bikers of all ability levels may use it. The Island Line Trail, which connects the Burlington riverfront to the Champlain Islands, is another popular riding destination. This 14-mile track features a cycle ferry that ferries bikers over a break in the causeway and gives views of the lake and the Green Mountains.

Another popular activity in and around Burlington is hiking. The Green Mountains, part of the Appalachian Mountain range, include a variety of hiking trails for people of all experience levels. The Camel's Hump Trail, with its top offering panoramic views of the surrounding terrain, is one of the most popular walks in the region. Those looking for a shorter climb might consider the Mount Philo Trail, which is just a 20-

minute drive from Burlington and provides views of Lake Champlain and the Adirondack Mountains.

Lake Champlain, which offers opportunities for swimming, boating, fishing, and paddleboarding, is extremely popular in Burlington. The Burlington Waterfront Park is a popular swimming and sunbathing destination, and there are various paddleboard and kayak rental choices. Various marinas in the vicinity provide boat rentals and charters for individuals who prefer powered water activities.

Skiing and snowboarding are popular winter activities in the Burlington area. A short drive from the city is various ski resorts, including Stowe Mountain Resort, Sugarbush Resort, and Bolton Valley Resort. These resorts provide a range of terrain for skiers and snowboarders of all ability levels, as well as ski and snowboard rentals and instruction for novices.

Burlington also offers several parks and environmental areas worth visiting. The Ethan Allen Homestead, just outside of town, has hiking trails and a historic farmhouse to visit. Another popular location is the Intervale Conservation Nursery and Farm, which has walking paths and a functioning farm that provides tours and classes.

Visitors visiting Burlington and the surrounding region will discover an abundance of outdoor activity opportunities. There's something for everyone in this gorgeous region of Vermont, whether you're an avid cyclist, hiker, water sports lover, or skier.

CHAPTER 4

ROAD TRIPS AND DAY TRIPS

Vermont is a small state with a lot of natural beauty and historical charm. Taking a road trip or a day trip to some of the state's most picturesque and intriguing places is one of the finest ways to experience the state. There's something for everyone, from meandering rural roads to beautiful tiny villages.

The Route 100 Scenic Byway, which runs north-south across the state's midsection, is one of the most popular road trips in Vermont. This 200-mile route winds through some of Vermont's most attractive towns and villages, as well as its breathtaking mountain scenery. Visitors may stop along the journey at small country stores, artisan shops, and historic attractions. The quaint town of Stowe, famous for its picturesque Main

Street, superb skiing, and gorgeous mountain views, is a must-see destination along Route 100.

The Northeast Kingdom Scenic Byway, which runs along the state's eastern border, is another popular road trip in Vermont. This 90-mile route passes through attractive small villages like St. Johnsbury and Lyndonville, as well as spectacular views of the Green Mountains and the Connecticut River. Along the journey, visitors may stop at picturesque viewpoints, historic sites, and hiking trails.

Shorter day trips are also available in Vermont for those who like them. Shelburne, a small village immediately south of Burlington, is a popular tourist destination. The Shelburne Museum is a one-of-a-kind collection of historic buildings, art, and artifacts that tell the narrative of Vermont's history. Tourists may also visit Shelburne Farms, a historic estate with guided tours, farm-to-table eating, and hiking trails.

Woodstock, situated in central Vermont, is another favorite day trip location. Woodstock is well-known for its beautiful covered bridges, picturesque downtown area, and breathtaking views of the Green Mountains. Tourists may visit the Billings Farm and Museum, a functioning farm that highlights Vermont's agricultural legacy, or trek to the summit of Mount Tom for panoramic views of the surrounding area.

A visit to the town of Waterbury is a must if you want to sample Vermont's famed maple syrup. The Ben & Jerry's Ice Cream Factory is located in Waterbury, where tourists may take a guided tour of the production and enjoy some of the company's renowned ice cream. Tourists may also visit the adjacent Cold Hollow Cider

Mill, which serves fresh cider doughnuts and other Vermont-made items.

A journey to the Mad River Valley is a must for individuals who like outdoor activity. This region, just south of Montpelier, is well-known for its great skiing and snowboarding, as well as hiking and mountain bike paths. The Mad River Byway, which passes through the center of the valley and provides spectacular views of the surrounding mountains, is a picturesque drive for visitors.

Vermont offers something for everyone, whether you're searching for a picturesque road trip or a quick day vacation. This state is a must-see for anybody who enjoys exploring, thanks to its charming small villages, spectacular natural beauty, and rich history.

VERMONT'S MOST SCENIC DRIVES

Vermont is recognized for its breathtaking natural beauty, and taking a scenic drive is one of the greatest ways to see it. Vermont's highways provide something for everyone, from twisting mountain routes to peaceful rural lanes. These are some of the most picturesque routes in Vermont that you won't want to miss.

Route 100: Route 100 is known as the "Skiers' Highway." Route 100 stretches from the Massachusetts border to the Canadian border in Vermont. You'll travel through charming towns and villages, picturesque countryside, and the Green Mountains along the route. The foliage along this road in the autumn is some of the nicest in the state.

Route 7: Stretching from Massachusetts to Canada, Route 7 passes through some of Vermont's most scenic little towns, including Manchester, Bennington, and Middlebury. You'll also see the historic houses and farms of the state's early settlers along the journey.

Smugglers' Notch: This narrow mountain pass connects Stowe and Jeffersonville and is one of Vermont's most picturesque routes. The route winds across the mountains, providing spectacular views of the surrounding scenery. The greenery is particularly beautiful in the autumn.

The Lake Champlain Islands: Situated in the state's northwest corner, the Lake Champlain Islands include some of Vermont's most magnificent landscapes. Take a leisurely drive around the islands to take in the views of the lake, the Adirondack Mountains, and Vermont's rolling countryside.

The Mad River Byway: This 36-mile picturesque journey takes you into Vermont's ski area, passing through Waitsfield, Warren, and Fayston. You'll see gorgeous rivers and streams, covered bridges, and attractive towns along the road.

The Molly Stark Trail: During the American Revolution, this historic trail followed the course of the Green Mountain Boys as they marched to fight. The route passes through some of Vermont's most beautiful scenery, including the Green Mountains and the Connecticut River Valley.

The Appalachian Gap: This mountain pass connects Warren and Huntington and provides some of Vermont's most breathtaking views. The route climbs the mountain, passing through dense forests and providing views of the surrounding scenery.

The Northeast Kingdom: Situated in the state's northeastern corner, the Northeast Kingdom is a remote and rocky area with some of Vermont's most magnificent landscapes. Take a drive around the region to see the vistas of the Green Mountains, the Connecticut River, and Vermont's rolling hills.

Whichever gorgeous route you select, take your time and appreciate the scenery. Vermont's natural beauty is genuinely distinctive, and these picturesque drives provide a unique way to appreciate it.

DAY TRIP IDEAS FROM BURLINGTON

Burlington, Vermont's biggest city, is a popular tourist destination due to its picturesque waterfront, lively downtown, and appealing small-town atmosphere. Although there is a lot to see and do in the city, there are also a lot of wonderful day trip alternatives for people who want to explore the surrounding region. These are some of the top Burlington day trip options.

Stowe: Famous for its world-class skiing and snowboarding, Stowe is a lovely town worth visiting at any time of year. Summer activities include hiking, mountain biking, and swimming at neighboring swimming holes. Take in the breathtaking autumn foliage. In the winter, take to the slopes at Stowe Ski Resort.

Shelburne: A lovely town just south of Burlington, Shelburne is recognized for its historic attractions, including the Shelburne Museum, which has art and artifacts from the 18th to the 20th centuries. Tourists may also visit the Shelburne Farms, a National Historic Landmark that has a functioning farm as well as walking paths.

Lake Champlain Islands: A trip north of Burlington will take you to the Lake Champlain Islands, a chain of islands with breathtaking views of Lake Champlain and the Adirondack Mountains. Explore the picturesque villages of South Hero and North Hero, which are famous for their beaches, farms, and vineyards, after taking a boat journey to the islands.

Middlebury: About 45 minutes south of Burlington, Middlebury is a charming college town worth visiting.

Visit Middlebury College, stroll through the town's various shops and restaurants, and explore neighboring Snake Mountain.

Montpelier: Vermont's capital city is about an hour's drive from Burlington and is a fantastic day trip. Visit the Vermont State House, walk around Hubbard Park, and explore the city's many art galleries and stores.

Ben & Jerry's Factory: Ice cream lovers will not want to miss a visit to the Ben & Jerry's Factory, which is situated about 45 minutes east of Burlington. Enjoy a factory tour, learn about the company's history, and, of course, have some wonderful ice cream.

Green Mountain National Forest: Vermont is recognized for its gorgeous beauty, and the Green

Mountain National Forest is no exception. The forest, which is about two hours south of Burlington, has miles of hiking trails, picturesque roads, and camping and fishing options.

Dartmouth College: Dartmouth College, one of the nation's most prestigious Ivy League colleges, is just over the border in Hanover, New Hampshire. Tourists may tour the campus, visit the Hood Museum of Art, and dine at one of the many restaurants and stores in downtown Hanover.

Whatever your hobbies are, Vermont has much to see and do. These Burlington day trip ideas are just a handful of the numerous possibilities accessible to travelers. Vermont has it all, whether you're seeking outdoor adventure, cultural events, or simply some time to rest and unwind.

ROAD TRIP ITINERARIES FOR ALL INTERESTS

Vermont, with its winding country roads, rolling hills, and magnificent scenery, is best experienced by car. There are road trip routes to suit any interest, whether you want to see the state's lovely small towns, natural treasures, or culinary scene.

Scenic Route 100

Route 100, which runs the length of the state from north to south, is one of the most popular scenic drives in Vermont. This route passes through some of Vermont's most beautiful towns, including Stowe, Killington, and Manchester. Along the journey, you'll drive through the Green Mountain National Forest and have the opportunity to pause for breathtaking views of the surrounding mountains and valleys. This trip is particularly popular in the autumn as the leaves change colors, but it's stunning any time of year.

Northeast Kingdom

The Northeast Kingdom is a lonely, rural area in the northeast corner of Vermont. This route passes through small towns and villages, rolling hills, and beautiful forests. Visit the Fairbanks Museum and Planetarium in St. Johnsbury, or go mountain biking or hiking on the Kingdom Trails. The trip up to Lake Willoughby is particularly beautiful, with views of the surrounding mountains and the lake's crystal-pure water.

Vermont Cheese Trail

Vermont is well-known for its cheese, and the Vermont Cheese Trail is a self-guided tour of some of the state's greatest cheesemakers. Almost 280 miles of gorgeous Vermont countryside are covered by the path, which includes stops at cheesemakers, farms, and businesses. You may try cheeses, learn about the cheesemaking process, and take home some tasty souvenirs.

Covered Bridges

Vermont is famous for its covered bridges, and this route takes you to some of the more well-known examples. Beginning in Bennington, you'll travel through the Green Mountains, stopping at historic bridges at Arlington, Woodstock, and Quechee. You may stop for a picnic or a hike in the woods along the way.

Lake Champlain Byway

The Lake Champlain Byway follows the lake's beaches, providing breathtaking views of the lake and neighboring mountains. You may start in Burlington and travel north to the Canadian border, stopping along the way at attractive lakeside villages and historic landmarks. Stop in Vergennes for lunch at the Basin Harbor Club, or take the boat to New York to enjoy the Adirondack Mountains.

Route 7

Route 7 is another well-known beautiful route that passes through some of Vermont's most lovely towns. Beginning in the south with Bennington, you'll drive through Manchester, Rutland, and Middlebury, among other places. You may stop along the road to see historic landmarks, art galleries, and lovely stores. The trip through the Green Mountains is particularly lovely, with views of the surrounding peaks and valleys.

Mad River Byway

The Mad River Byway is a picturesque drive through the Green Mountains that follows the Mad River.

You'll travel through the small villages of Waitsfield and Warren along the way, where you may visit art galleries and antique stores. The trail goes through the Mad River Glen ski resort, which is recognized for its difficult terrain and old-school vibe.

Whichever road trip plan you select, Vermont's breathtaking countryside and lovely small towns will not disappoint. Take in the scenery, sample the local food, and interact with the friendly residents along the way.

CHAPTER 5

VERMONT FOR FAMILIES

Vermont is an excellent place for families wishing to spend quality time together and make lasting memories. From outdoor adventures to cultural experiences, the state has a vast choice of activities to keep both kids and adults engaged. Let's look at some of Vermont's top family-friendly activities and places.

Outdoor Adventures

Vermont's natural beauty offers the ideal background for family-friendly outdoor activities. There are several options to go outdoors and explore, whether you want to walk, bike, swim, or paddle.

The Green Mountain National Forest is a popular location, with miles of hiking and bike routes, as well as camping and picnic spots. The park has several beautiful waterfalls, including Moss Glen Falls and Lye Brook Falls, which are great for a family hike.

Lake Champlain, on the border of Vermont and New York, is another fantastic place for outdoor fun. Swimming, fishing, and kayaking are popular activities for families, as is a scenic boat trip to the lake.

Museums and Cultural Experiences

Vermont also has several museums and cultural activities that are suitable for families. The Shelburne Museum, just outside of Burlington, is a must-see attraction. The museum has 45 acres of gardens, historic structures, and exhibits showcasing American art and design.

The ECHO Leahy Center for Lake Champlain, an interactive science and nature museum with hands-on exhibits and events for all ages, is another fantastic destination for families. The museum includes a four-story aquarium, a touch tank with real marine animals, and displays about Lake Champlain's ecology and history.

Farm Experiences

Vermont is well-known for its picturesque farms, many of which provide family-friendly activities and experiences. The Billings Farm & Museum in Woodstock is a real dairy farm that provides everyday activities for families such as cow milking, animal feeding, and wagon rides.

Shelburne Farms, which provides tours of its historic mansion, gardens, and working farm, is another famous farm experience. Families may also participate in instructional activities like cheesemaking and maple sugaring.

Winter Sports

Winter is a lovely time in Vermont, and families may enjoy a range of winter sports activities such as skiing, snowboarding, snowshoeing, and ice skating. Stowe Mountain Resort, Sugarbush Resort, and Okemo Mountain Resort are among the state's ski resorts.

Cross-country skiing and snowshoeing may also be enjoyed by families in one of the state parks or nature reserves. With its scenic trails and ponds, the Catamount Outdoor Family Center in Williston provides cross-country skiing, snowshoeing, and ice skating.

Festivals and Special Events

Throughout the year, Vermont organizes several festivals and events that are suitable for families. Families may enjoy the Vermont Pumpkin Chuckin' Festival in the autumn, where participants create and launch handmade pumpkin cannons. In the spring, the Vermont Maple Festival celebrates the state's famed maple syrup with cuisine, music, and demonstrations.

Families may enjoy the Champlain Valley Fair, a traditional county fair with carnival rides, games, and animal events, throughout the summer. With jousting tournaments, costumed entertainers, and medieval crafts, the Vermont Renaissance Faire, held in August, takes visitors back in time.

Vermont has a variety of family-friendly activities and attractions that are guaranteed to leave a memorable impression. Vermont offers something for everyone, whether you want to explore the great outdoors, learn about history and culture, or just have fun.

FAMILY-FRIENDLY ACTIVITIES AND ATTRACTIONS

Vermont is well-known for its outdoor activities and cultural experiences, but it is also an excellent family vacation. There are lots of family-friendly activities and places to enjoy around the state, whether you're traveling with small children or teenagers. Vermont provides something for everyone in the family, from outdoor adventures to educational experiences.

Skiing and snowboarding are two of the most popular family-friendly activities in Vermont. Families can spend a day on the slopes together thanks to the state's several ski resorts. Several resorts provide ski instruction and childcare services, allowing families to enjoy the slopes while their children are being cared for. If skiing isn't your thing, there are lots of alternative outdoor activities to do with your family. Vermont features several state parks and national forests with hiking paths, picnic spots, and wildlife viewing locations. Throughout the summer, families may also enjoy fishing and swimming in Vermont's various lakes and rivers.

Vermont offers various museums and historic places to visit for families searching for an educational experience. The ECHO Leahy Center for Lake Champlain in Burlington is a fun science and nature museum for kids of all ages. Another famous destination in Shelburne is the Shelburne Museum, which features art, history, and gardens.

Families may also learn about Vermont agriculture by visiting local farms and taking farm tours. Several farms provide tours where families may learn about sustainable farming practices, select fruits and vegetables, and even meet the animals. Kids will enjoy getting up and personal with farm animals and learning about where their food comes from.

Visiting Vermont's many maple sugar houses is another favorite family activity. Family may learn about maple syrup production and taste fresh, pure maple syrup from the source. Maple-themed food and items, such as maple candy and maple cream, are available in many sugar houses.

Family may also enjoy one of Vermont's many fairs and festivals. Both the Vermont State Fair in Rutland and the Champlain Valley Fair in Essex Junction are popular family-friendly festivals that include rides, games, cuisine, and entertainment. Other famous events that highlight Vermont's culinary specialties include the Vermont Maple Festival in St. Albans and the Vermont Cheese Festival in Shelburne.

Vermont offers a variety of adventurous activities for families with older kids or teenagers. Zipline, rock climbing, and mountain biking are just a few of the exciting activities available around the state. Kayaking and canoeing are some other popular activities for families in Vermont's lakes and rivers.

When it comes to accommodation, Vermont has a variety of family-friendly options. Several hotels and resorts have family suites or connected rooms to enable families to remain together. Some resorts even include activities and programs just for kids, such as arts and crafts or nature hikes. Renting a vacation house or cabin is another popular choice for families. Vermont offers a wide range of rental accommodations, from quiet cottages in the woods to spacious homes with plenty of space for the whole family. Renting a vacation home may also be a cost-effective alternative since families can save money by preparing meals at home rather than dining out.

Vermont is an excellent family vacation spot. There is something for everyone in the family to enjoy with its natural beauty, educational experiences, and diverse choice of activities. Vermont offers it all, whether you're seeking for outdoor adventures or cultural experiences.

KID-FRIENDLY DINING AND ACCOMMODATIONS

Vermont is an excellent family vacation, with several activities and attractions for children of all ages. While planning a family trip in Vermont, keep in mind kid-friendly dining options and accommodations that will make everyone feel at ease.

Let's start with the dining options. Vermont is famous for its farm-to-table cuisine, which means that many of the state's restaurants employ locally produced products to make tasty and nutritious meals. This is an excellent alternative for families who want to guarantee that their children eat fresh and healthy meals while on vacation. Several restaurants now provide children's menus or smaller portions of adult dishes.

The Skinny Pancake, which serves a selection of crepes and other breakfast dishes that are likely to suit even the pickiest eaters, is one of Vermont's finest kid-friendly eateries. Another fantastic choice is the Farmhouse Tap & Grill in Burlington, which serves burgers, mac and cheese, and other classic comfort meals. The Kitchen Table Restaurant in Richmond provides gluten-free and vegetarian alternatives for families with dietary requirements.

There are several family-friendly accommodations available around the state. Swimming pools, playgrounds, and gaming rooms are common attractions at hotels and resorts, as are activities such as nature walks and arts and crafts classes. Vermont features a variety of campsites and cottages that are ideal for a nature-filled vacation for families who desire a more rustic experience.

The Jay Peak Resort, which provides skiing, water parks, and other activities all year, is one of Vermont's best family-friendly accommodations. Families may pick from a variety of lodging options at the resort, including hotel rooms, suites, and townhouses. Another popular option is the Smugglers' Notch Resort, which has a zip line, a climbing wall, and an indoor pool.

Vermont has a variety of family-friendly activities and places to enjoy. These are some of my favorites:

Shelburne Museum: This museum is great for teaching children about Vermont's history and culture. It has a carousel and a train ride, as well as exhibitions such as historic buildings, artwork, and artifacts.

Lake Champlain Maritime Museum: Situated in Vergennes, this museum provides hands-on displays and events that explore Lake Champlain's history and environment. Kids may go on a pirate treasure hunt, learn how to paddle a boat, and much more.

Ben & Jerry's Factory Tour: This famous Waterbury site takes visitors behind the scenes to see how Ben & Jerry's ice cream is created. Children may try various varieties, go on a guided tour, and even manufacture their ice cream.

Vermont Teddy Bear Company: This Shelburne manufacturer makes handcrafted teddy bears that are popular with both children and adults. Visitors may take a factory tour, manufacture their bear, and even dress it up in various clothing.

Adventure parks: Many adventure parks in Vermont provide activities such as zip lining, ropes courses, and rock climbing. ArborTrek Canopy Adventures in Jeffersonville and Bromley Mountain Adventure Park in Peru are two of the best parks.

Vermont provides plenty for families of all ages, whether they are searching for outdoor adventures, cultural experiences, or simply a quiet holiday. Vermont is a terrific spot to make lasting experiences with your loved ones because of its natural beauty, friendly locals, and emphasis on sustainable living.

TIPS FOR TRAVELING WITH KIDS IN VERMONT

Vermont is an excellent choice for families searching for outdoor activities, beautiful landscapes, and a laid-back environment. Traveling with children may be a lot of fun, but it also needs careful planning to ensure that everyone has a good time. Here are some ideas for family vacations in Vermont.

Plan your itinerary carefully

Be sure to include lots of kid-friendly activities on your agenda when planning a trip to Vermont. Hiking, swimming, visiting museums, and attending events and festivals are all possibilities. Make time for leisure as well, so that everyone has a chance to relax and recharge.

Choose family-friendly accommodations

Vermont has a variety of family-friendly accommodation options, including hotels, motels, and vacation rentals. Search for residences that include features like swimming pools, playgrounds, and family-friendly restaurants. You may also wish to choose a site near the activities you have planned.

Pack for all kinds of weather

Vermont may have a broad variety of weather conditions, so bring clothes for all scenarios. Layering is essential since temperatures may change dramatically from day to night. Bring sunscreen, insect repellent, and caps to keep your family safe from the sun.

Embrace the outdoors

Vermont is recognized for its stunning natural environment, so spend as much time as possible outside with your family. There are several hiking trails, swimming holes, and parks to visit. Hire bikes, go kayaking or canoeing, or just enjoy the surroundings by taking a leisurely drive.

Check out the local farmers' markets

Vermont has a variety of farmers' markets where you may taste fresh vegetables and other locally produced items. Several of these markets also include live music and other entertainment, making them a wonderful family experience.

Attend local events and festivals

During the year, Vermont hosts a variety of events and festivals, many of which are family-friendly. Check out the local events calendar to discover what's going on during your stay. The Vermont Maple Festival, the Stowe Winter Carnival, and the Ben & Jerry's Concerts on the Green are all popular events.

Take advantage of family-friendly discounts

Several sites and activities in Vermont offer family discounts, so inquire about them when you reserve your tickets. You could also consider family packages or passes that provide savings on several attractions.

Keep everyone well-fed

Children might get cranky when they are hungry, so keep them well-fed on your travel. Search for family-friendly restaurants with a diverse menu that includes healthful selections. Include food and beverages for lengthy vehicle journeys and outdoor activities as well.

Be flexible

Traveling with children requires flexibility since you never know when someone will get weary or grumpy. Prepare to change your plans as required and take pauses as needed. Remember that the purpose is to have fun and build memories, so don't worry about keeping to a strict schedule.

Have a good time!

Above all, remember to have fun! Vermont is an excellent family vacation location, with lots of chances for both action and leisure. Take plenty of pictures, explore new activities, and enjoy your family time together.

CHAPTER 6

SUSTAINABLE VERMONT

Vermont takes pride in being ecologically conscious and environmentally sustainable. It's no surprise that Vermonters care deeply about preserving their land and resources for future generations, given the state's tremendous natural beauty. We'll look at what makes Vermont a sustainable destination and how tourists may participate in responsible travel.

Vermont's commitment to sustainability starts with agriculture. Visitors may buy fresh fruit and locally created items at the state's organic farms and farmers' markets. In addition, the state boasts a thriving craft beer and cider sector, with many brewers and cideries obtaining their ingredients locally. Visitors may help minimize their carbon footprint by patronizing local businesses, which reduces the need for long-distance transportation of products. Visitors may support local businesses while making environmentally friendly transportation choices. Vermont has an extensive public transportation system that includes buses and trains, making it possible to explore the state without a vehicle. Those who choose to drive will find hybrid and electric car charging stations around the state.

Participating in outdoor activities that promote conservation and environmental education is another option to enjoy Vermont sustainably. Hiking, kayaking, and other outdoor activities are available in the state's parks and natural regions, and they may be enjoyed while learning about the state's animals and natural resources. Several of these locations provide educational programs and guided tours that educate visitors on the value of conservation and sustainable practices.

Tourists may also pick environmentally friendly hotel options. Vermont offers an extensive range of eco-friendly lodging options, including bed & breakfasts, motels, and campsites that use renewable energy, recycle, and reduce waste. Some housing alternatives even offer environmentally friendly features such as solar panels or green roofs.

Vermont is likewise devoted to living sustainably. The state has set a target of reaching 90% renewable energy by 2050 and has launched many efforts to that end. The Clean Energy Development Fund, for example, offers money for renewable energy projects around the state.

Vermont's dedication to sustainability makes it an ideal location for those looking to make responsible decisions and learn about sustainable living. Visitors may support local businesses, use sustainable transportation, engage in conservation and environmental education programs, and stay in eco-friendly hotels. Visitors may help protect Vermont's natural beauty and resources for future generations by doing so.

ECO-FRIENDLY TOURISM IN VERMONT

Vermont takes pride in its dedication to sustainability and environmental responsibility. As a result, many tourists to the state are interested in eco-friendly tourism choices that enable them to minimize their ecological impact while still enjoying all Vermont has to offer. Thankfully, there are several possibilities to do so.

Exploring Vermont's various hiking trails is one of the finest ways to enjoy the state's natural beauty while being environmentally conscious. There are several possibilities for hikers of all ability levels, ranging from the Long Trail, which runs the length of the state, to smaller trails in state parks and nature preserves. Hiking, in addition to offering exercise and fresh air, enables tourists to get up and personal with Vermont's flora and animals while causing no damage to the environment.

Exploring the state's rivers by kayak or canoe is another fantastic eco-friendly option in Vermont. Paddling is ideal on Vermont's various lakes and rivers, as well as a piece of Lake Champlain. Kayaking and canoeing, in addition to being a fun activity for families and groups, enable tourists to view Vermont's natural beauty from a unique perspective while causing no damage to the environment.

Cycling is a terrific eco-friendly choice in Vermont for individuals who want to remain on the land. The state includes a vast network of bike routes, including the Burlington Greenway, which follows Lake Champlain's shoreline, and the Island Line Trail, which stretches from Burlington to South Hero. Biking is a terrific way to get some exercise while enjoying Vermont's picturesque countryside, plus it produces no emissions, making it an ecologically friendly option.

Vermont also has a variety of eco-friendly hotel alternatives. There are several places to stay that are devoted to sustainability, ranging from bed & breakfasts to rustic cottages. Some lodgings employ sustainable energy sources such as solar or wind power, while others have recycling initiatives or serve organic, locally produced cuisine.

Vermont's environmental concern goes beyond its outdoor activities and hotel alternatives. T the state has a vibrant farm-to-table movement, with many restaurants purchasing products from local farmers and food producers. Visitors may support sustainable agriculture and lower their carbon footprint by eating at restaurants that prioritize locally produced organic cuisine.

Tourists may also learn more about sustainability by visiting some of Vermont's eco-friendly sites. For example, the Shelburne Farms Historic Inn and Property is a functioning farm that provides tours and educational programs about sustainable agriculture and land management. The ECHO Leahy Center for Lake Champlain, with exhibits and educational activities focusing on the lake's ecology and conservation, is another fantastic location for eco-conscious tourists.

Visitors may help the environment by being conscious of their behaviors while in Vermont. Conserving water and energy, using public transit or bicycling instead of driving, and properly disposing of waste and recycling are all examples of this. Visitors may help preserve Vermont's natural beauty for future generations by making small changes to their everyday activities.

Eco-friendly tourism is a fantastic alternative for Vermont tourists who wish to limit their environmental impact while enjoying all the state has to offer. From hiking and kayaking to biking and dining at farm-to-table restaurants, there are several ways to enjoy Vermont's natural beauty while being environmentally conscious. Visitors may help guarantee that Vermont remains a beautiful and thriving destination for years to come by making simple adjustments to their daily routines and supporting companies and attractions that promote sustainability.

SUSTAINABLE LODGING AND DINING OPTIONS

As more people become conscious of the environmental effect of travel, sustainable tourism has grown in popularity. Vermont, famous for its magnificent natural beauty and dedication to environmental protection, is an ideal location for eco-conscious travelers. We'll look at the top environmentally friendly hotel and eating alternatives in Vermont.

Sustainable Lodging:

The Inn at Shelburne Farms: Located on a 1,400-acre working farm, this historic inn is dedicated to sustainability. The inn serves organic and locally produced meals, and the facility includes a biomass boiler and solar panels to provide sustainable energy.

The Pitcher Inn: This Warren luxury inn is dedicated to sustainability and has earned Vermont Business Environmental Partner accreditation. 275 Main, the inn's restaurant, seeks local foods and provides a farm-to-table dining experience.

Topnotch Resort: This Stowe resort is dedicated to sustainability and has received the Green Business accreditation. The resort provides energy-efficient guest accommodations, food made from locally produced ingredients, and a range of eco-friendly activities.

Hotel Vermont: This Burlington boutique hotel is devoted to sustainability and has obtained LEED Gold accreditation. The hotel serves locally produced cuisine and provides visitors with bicycles to explore the city.

The Lodge at Spruce Peak: This luxury resort in Stowe is devoted to sustainability and has gained Audubon International's Green Leaf Eco-Rating accreditation. The resort has energy-efficient guest rooms and makes an effort to source local, sustainable products for its restaurants.

Sustainable Dining:

Revolution Kitchen: This Burlington restaurant is devoted to sustainability and sources local and organic ingredients. Vegan and gluten-free alternatives are also available at the restaurant.

The Skinny Pancake: With outlets in Burlington, Montpelier, and Hanover, New Hampshire, this local business is dedicated to sourcing locally, organically, and sustainably grown foods. All waste is composted and recycled at the restaurants.

Hen of the Wood: With locations in Burlington and Waterbury, this restaurant is devoted to sustainability and obtains products from local farmers and suppliers. In addition, the restaurant composts all food waste and recycles all materials.

American Flatbread: This Burlington and Middlebury-based restaurant is devoted to sustainability and gets organic ingredients from local farmers. All waste is composted and recycled at the restaurants.

Prohibition Pig: This Waterbury eatery uses local and sustainable foods and recycles all waste. The restaurant is dedicated to reducing its environmental footprint.

Visiting responsibly in Vermont is simple, given the state's environmental dedication and variety of environmentally friendly hotel and dining options. You can enjoy everything that Vermont has to offer while limiting your environmental impact by selecting eco-friendly lodging and dining businesses.

LOCAL INITIATIVES TO PROTECT VERMONT'S ENVIRONMENT

Vermont is well-known for its natural beauty and pristine atmosphere. It should come as no surprise that the state is home to an array of projects aimed at safeguarding the environment and promoting sustainability. We'll look more closely at some of these programs and how they contribute to Vermont's status as a top destination for eco-friendly tourism.

Vermont's dedication to renewable energy is one of its most visible efforts. Vermont is one of the nation's leaders in renewable energy generation, to source 90% of its energy from renewable sources by 2050. The state's dedication to renewable energy is seen in the landscape, with several wind and solar farms dotting the area. Visitors visiting Vermont may see firsthand the state's commitment to sustainable energy and learn about the different carbon-reduction projects.

Vermont also excels in the agriculture business when it comes to sustainability. Dairy farms in the state are known for their environmentally friendly techniques, such as rotational grazing and the use of energy from renewable sources. Moreover, Vermont is home to a large number of small-scale organic farms that specialize in a range of crops. Guests may enjoy farm-to-table dining experiences and see the sustainable agricultural techniques that have helped Vermont become a model for sustainable agriculture.

Vermont's commitment to environmental conservation is also reflected in the state's wide network of state parks and protected areas. The state has nearly 50 state parks, each dedicated to conserving the natural beauty and supporting sustainable tourist practices. Several of these parks enable visitors to camp and hike, enabling them to completely immerse themselves in the state's natural landscape. Moreover, the state is home to various wilderness areas, including the Green Mountain National Forest and the Northeast Kingdom, which give tourists even more opportunities to interact with nature and experience Vermont's dedication to environmental conservation.

Another facet of Vermont's sustainable tourism is the state's emphasis on local and sustainable tourist efforts. Several Vermont companies are dedicated to using local goods and promoting sustainable tourist practices. Visitors may help these programs by shopping at companies that value sustainability and environmental preservation. There are several ways to promote sustainable tourism in Vermont, ranging from locally produced farm-to-table restaurants to eco-friendly accommodation options.

Vermont is also home to several environmental groups committed to the preservation of the state's natural resources. Conservation activities and advocacy work are done by organizations such as the Vermont Natural Resources Council and the Lake Champlain Committee to conserve the state's forests, lakes, and rivers. Visitors visiting the state may learn more about these organizations and their activities by participating in educational programs and volunteering.

Vermont is a leader in sustainable transportation efforts, promoting the use of public transportation and alternate forms of transportation. The state has a vast network of bike routes, pedestrian walkways, and public transit choices, making it simple for tourists to explore the state without depending on cars. Moreover, many of the state's tourist enterprises provide environmentally friendly mobility choices, such as electric vehicle rentals and bike rentals, enabling visitors to reduce their carbon footprint while visiting the state.

Vermont is a model for environmentally friendly tourism and environmental conservation. Vermont is committed to conserving its natural beauty and supporting sustainable tourist practices, from its dedication to renewable energy to its sustainable agricultural methods and wide network of state parks. Visitors may help support these programs by shopping at companies that promote sustainability and using the state's various eco-friendly transportation alternatives. Visitors may help to guarantee that Vermont remains a top destination for sustainable tourism for future generations by doing so.

CHAPTER 7

PRACTICAL INFORMATION

Vermont is a lovely state with a distinct charm and personality that attracts travelers from all over the world. If you're planning a vacation to Vermont, you must have all of the necessary information to make your stay as pleasurable as possible. Here are some pointers and ideas to help you organize your trip.

Climate and Weather

Vermont has four different seasons, each with its own set of weather patterns. Summer temperatures typically range from the mid-60s to the mid-80s. The most popular season to visit Vermont is in the fall when the leaf colors are magnificent. Winters are very cold and snowy, with temperatures often falling below freezing. Spring might be cold and rainy, but it is also a more peaceful season to visit.

How to Get There

Vermont may be reached by car, bus, or air. Burlington International Airport (BTV) and Rutland Southern Vermont Regional Airport are the two main airports (RUT). Amtrak also serves Vermont by train, including stations in Rutland and Waterbury. If you're driving, Vermont is accessible through major roads such as Interstates 89 and 91.

Getting Around

Vermont is a relatively small state, so getting around is easy. The best method to see the state is by vehicle since there are several lovely drives across the countryside. There are also several bike routes and walking pathways that are ideal for experiencing the state's natural splendor.

Lodging

Vermont provides a broad choice of hotel alternatives to accommodate all budgets and interests. There's something for everyone, from cozy bed and breakfasts to luxurious resorts. Moreover, several of the state's campsites and state parks include rustic camping options for individuals who like to rough it.

Dining

Vermont is well-known for its delectable farm-to-table cuisine made from fresh, locally sourced ingredients. Throughout the state, several outstanding restaurants and cafés provide a variety of eating choices ranging from casual to upscale.

Shopping

Vermont shopping is also a terrific area to get locally created goods such as maple syrup, cheese, and handmade crafts. Several small communities around the state have lovely stores and boutiques where you may discover one-of-a-kind items and souvenirs.

Safety

Vermont is typically a safe destination to visit, but you should always take care to protect your safety. While parking in public locations, always be careful to secure your vehicle and keep valuables out of sight. Be aware of your surroundings and avoid going alone at night in strange areas.

Sustainability

Vermont is dedicated to conserving its natural beauty for future generations. Use reusable water bottles, recycle, and choose eco-friendly housing and transportation alternatives while visiting Vermont to reduce your environmental impact.

Language

Vermont's official language is English, however, French is widely spoken in some parts of the state, especially along the Canadian border.

Currency

The Vermont dollar is the official currency. Most stores take credit cards, but carrying cash is usually a smart idea, particularly when visiting smaller towns and shops.

Vermont is a lovely and distinct state with something for everyone. Vermont is likely to provide whether you're seeking outdoor adventure, cultural events, or a quiet break. You may assure a memorable and pleasurable journey to the Green Mountain State by following these practical ideas and recommendations.

ESSENTIAL TRAVEL TIPS

Vermont is a lovely state that has much to offer to all sorts of tourists. Vermont has something for everyone, from picturesque drives to outdoor pursuits and charming small villages. Whether you're a first-time visitor or a seasoned traveler, there are a few essential travel suggestions to help you make the most of your vacation to Vermont.

Plan ahead

Although Vermont is a small state, there is enough to see and do. It is important to prepare your itinerary ahead of time so that you do not miss out on any must-see locations or events. Create a list of your main priorities and plan your journey around them. Be sure to allow some flexibility in your schedule to take advantage of unforeseen chances or weather changes.

Dress appropriately for the weather

Vermont has four different seasons, each with its unique set of weather patterns and temperatures. Temperatures may dip below freezing in the winter, and snow is typical. Summer temperatures may reach the upper 80s and 90s. It is critical to dress correctly for the weather and pack layers that may be added or removed as required.

Wear comfy shoes.

Whether you're touring Vermont's lovely downtowns or hitting the trails for a trek, wear comfortable shoes that can handle any terrain. Vermont's terrain is tough and diverse, so be sure your footwear is up to the challenge.

Try the local cuisine

Vermont is well-known for its farm-to-table cuisine, handcrafted beer, and artisanal cheeses. During your stay, try some of the local specialties. Farmers' markets and local restaurants provide everything from maple syrup to grass-fed meat to fresh produce.

Environmental sensitivity

Vermont is a state that takes its environmental responsibilities seriously. Whether you're hiking in the Green Mountains or taking a beautiful drive, it's crucial to respect the state's natural beauty. Pack out any trash and avoid upsetting any animal or plant life.

Drive with care on rural roads

The scenic rural roads of Vermont may be narrow and winding, so drive with care. Keep an eye out for animals crossing the road and obey the speed limit. You could also come across farm trucks or other slow-moving traffic, so be patient and allow them plenty of space.

Carry cash

Although credit cards are commonly accepted in Vermont, several small establishments still take only cash. Carry some cash, particularly if you want to visit small towns or rural areas.

Make use of local resources.

Vermont has a variety of tourist centers and tourism bureaus where you may get useful information about the state. These websites may assist you in planning your itinerary, locating hotel and dining alternatives, and learning more about the history and culture of the state.

By following this vital travel advice, you can make the most of your vacation to Vermont and enjoy all that this lovely state has to offer. Vermont will captivate your heart and leave you with memories that will last a lifetime, whether you are a nature lover, a foodie, or a history enthusiast.

SAFETY ADVICE

Vermont has a low crime rate and pleasant towns, making it a reasonably safe state. And still, like with any holiday location, some care must be taken to guarantee your safety while enjoying everything that the state has to offer.

Weather-related occurrences are one of the most
serious safety problems in Vermont. Winters in the
state are cold and snowy, with occasional extreme
weather events like as thunderstorms and hurricanes.
Visitors should be informed of the weather prediction
and make appropriate plans. It's also a good idea to
dress appropriately for any outside activity, particularly
in the winter when temperatures may fall far below
freezing.

Vermont is well-known for its scenic beauty and
outdoor adventure opportunities. It is important to be
mindful of possible dangers when participating in these
activities. Hiking trails may be steep and rocky, and
river and lake currents can be strong. Stay on
designated trails, obey posted signs and cautions, and
never attempt activities that are above your ability
level.

Visitors should be careful of the state's meandering rural roads and narrow bridges while traveling in Vermont. It is critical to driving slowly, particularly in severe weather, and to be prepared for interactions with animals such as moose or deer.

Being alert of possible scams or fraud is another crucial component of being secure in Vermont. Unsolicited phone calls, emails, or other communications requesting personal information or financial transactions should be avoided. Before supplying sensitive information or making payments, it is critical to confirm the veracity of any request.

In the event of an emergency, it is critical to have an accurate identity and medical information readily accessible. Visitors should bring a copy of their passport or other identification, as well as any necessary medical information or prescription drugs, with them.

Visitors should be aware of the contact information for local emergency services, such as police, fire, and medical services, in the case of an emergency. 911 is the statewide emergency number.

Visitors may enjoy everything that Vermont has to offer while being safe and secure by adopting simple safety procedures and being aware of possible threats.

DRIVING IN VERMONT

Vermont is a small state recognized for its scenic beauty, rural charm, and charming communities. Whether you're a first-time visitor or a seasoned tourist, driving about Vermont is a great way to uncover its hidden jewels. Driving in Vermont, on the other hand, requires some planning and understanding of the state's roads, weather conditions, and driving rules. This section will offer you important information and driving safety advice for driving in Vermont.

Roads and scenery

Vermont boasts some of the most beautiful roads in the nation, and traveling through its mountains, valleys, and forests is a sensory joy. Vermont's roads, on the other hand, may be difficult to navigate. The state's highways and back roads vary from vast and level to narrow and winding. Some of Vermont's most popular scenic drives include:

- The Green Mountain Byway: An 11-mile road into the center of the Green Mountains with breathtaking views of Mount Mansfield and Smugglers' Notch.

- Route 100: A 200-mile route that travels through the heart of Vermont, passing through some of the state's most picturesque towns and villages.
- The Mad River Byway: A 36-mile circle across the Mad River Valley with breathtaking views of the Green Mountains, covered bridges, and picturesque waterfalls.

It is important to study your route and check for road closures and construction projects while planning a road trip to Vermont. The weather in Vermont may also have an impact on road conditions, particularly during the winter months. Check weather forecasts and traffic conditions before embarking on your journey.

Driving Laws

Vermont's driving rules are comparable to those of other states, however, there are a few differences to be aware of:

- Seat Belts: Seat belts are required in Vermont for all passengers in a vehicle, regardless of age or seating position.
- Child Safety Seats: Children under the age of eight or weighing less than 80 pounds are required by Vermont law to ride in a federally authorized child safety seat.
- Hands-Free Devices: Vermont law forbids drivers from using handheld electronic devices, such as mobile phones and GPS systems, while driving. To make calls or navigate, drivers may use hands-free gadgets or one-touch features.
- Slow Vehicles: Slow-moving vehicles, such as farm equipment or construction trucks, are

required by Vermont law to pull over and allow other cars to pass when it is safe to do so.

Speed Limits

The speed limits in Vermont vary based on the kind of road and location. The speed limit on rural roads is generally 50 mph, whereas the limit on interstates is 65 mph. Nevertheless, certain regions, particularly in residential or school zones, may have reduced speed restrictions. Keep an eye out for speed limit signs and adjust your driving appropriately.

Weather Conditions

The weather in Vermont may vary rapidly and drastically, particularly during the winter. Snow, ice, and freezing rain may all contribute to dangerous driving conditions, so it's critical to prepare your car for winter driving. Before you hit the road, be sure to:

- Check your tires: Check that your tires have enough tread and are properly inflated.
- Pack emergency supplies: In case of an emergency, bring blankets, food, drink, and a first-aid kit.
- Clear snow and ice from your car: Before driving, clear any snow and ice from your car's windows, roof, and hood.

It's also a good idea to check weather forecasts and traffic conditions before embarking on your journey.

Gas Stations

Vermont has an abundance of gas stations, so you should have no problem locating one when you need one. Nevertheless, since petrol stations may be few in certain rural areas, it is a good idea to plan and top up your tank before going on your excursion.

~ 168 ~

Another consideration while traveling in Vermont is the weather. Driving in winter weather conditions may be challenging, particularly if you are not used to driving on snow or ice. Before embarking on a winter road journey, make careful to check the weather forecast and road conditions. It's also a good idea to have snow tires or chains on hand, as well as emergency supplies like blankets, food, and water in case you are stuck or stranded.

One of the best parts about traveling in Vermont is the breathtaking landscape you'll see along the road. The state is well-known for its beautiful covered bridges, rolling hills, and small villages. Road 100, which extends from the Massachusetts border to the Canadian border, is a must-see. This route passes through some of Vermont's most picturesque towns and villages, as well as gorgeous mountains and lakes.

The Mad River Byway, which travels through the Mad River Valley and gives stunning views of the Green Mountains, is another gorgeous drive. You'll travel through charming towns, ancient covered bridges, and scenic countryside along the route. During the autumn foliage season, when the leaves change spectacular colors of red, orange, and yellow, this drive is very popular.

Consider taking the Ethan Allen Trail if you are interested in history. This path was used by Ethan Allen and the Green Mountain Boys during the Revolutionary War. You'll pass through historic landmarks like the Bennington Battle Monument and the Ethan Allen House along the route.

Driving in Vermont may be a joyful and rewarding experience if you take the proper precautions and prepare ahead of time. Vermont is ideal for a road trip because of its beautiful countryside and charming villages.

USEFUL CONTACTS AND WEBSITES

It is usually nice to have some useful contacts and websites to refer to while arranging a vacation to Vermont. Here, we will present you with some important resources to help you with your vacation planning.

Vermont Department of Tourism and Marketing

The Vermont Department of Tourism and Marketing is the state's official tourist agency. Their website, www.vermontvacation.com, is a one-stop shop for everything in Vermont. You may discover information about housing, restaurants, activities, events, and other topics here. You may also phone a toll-free hotline (1-800-VERMONT) for travel information.

Vermont State Parks

Vermont features a variety of state parks that provide opportunities for camping, hiking, swimming, and other outdoor activities. The Vermont State Parks website (www.vtstateparks.com) has information on each park, such as amenities, activities, and fees.

Vermont Farm to Plate

Vermont Farm to Plate is a statewide food system plan that seeks to increase agricultural and food-related economic growth. Their website (www.vtfarmtoplate.com) lists farmers' markets, food festivals, and other culinary events throughout Vermont.

Vermont Association of Snow Travelers (VAST)

Vermont Association of Snow Travelers (VAST) is a great resource if you're planning a winter vacation to Vermont. They manage approximately 5,000 miles of snowmobile trails throughout Vermont, and their website (www.vtvast.org) includes trail conditions, maps, and safety instructions.

Green Mountain Club

The Green Mountain Club is in charge of preserving Vermont's Long Trail, which runs the length of the state. Their website (www.greenmountainclub.org) has information about hiking the Long Trail as well as other hiking routes in the state.

Vermont Agency of Transportation

The website of the Vermont Agency of Transportation (www.aot.state.vt.us) offers information on road conditions, construction projects, and traffic updates. This is especially essential if you want to drive in Vermont.

Vermont League of Cities and Towns

The website of the Vermont League of Cities and Towns (www.vlct.org) has information about local government and services across the state. This might be handy if you need to contact a local government agency or learn about upcoming events in your area.

Vermont Department of Health

The website of the Vermont Department of Health (www.healthvermont.gov) offers information about health and safety concerns in the state. If you need to locate a doctor or hospital, or if you have issues regarding health and safety rules, this might be helpful.

Checking internet reviews for housing, restaurants, and activities is always a smart idea. Websites like TripAdvisor and Yelp may give useful information to other travelers. Having relevant connections and resources at your disposal may make the vacation preparation process go much more smoothly. These sites may give you with the knowledge you need to make the most of your Vermont trip, from the official tourist agency to groups that preserve Vermont's trails and parks.

APPENDIX

This section contains extra resources and information for Vermont visitors planning a vacation.

Vermont State Parks

Vermont offers a large network of state parks that provide a variety of recreational opportunities such as hiking, fishing, swimming, and camping. Among the most popular state parks are:

- Green River Reservoir State Park
- Lake Carmi State Park
- Lake St. Catherine State Park
- Little River State Park
- Mt. Philo State Park
- Quechee State Park

- Smugglers' Notch State Park
- Underhill State Park
- Vermont State Parks may be visited at https://vtstateparks.com/.

Vermont Events Calendar

Vermont's events calendar is usually brimming with fascinating activities such as festivals, concerts, and fairs. Among the popular events are:

- Burlington Discover Jazz Festival (June)
- Vermont Brewers Festival (July)
- Vermont Maple Festival (April)
- Champlain Valley Fair (August-September)
- Stowe Foliage Arts Festival (October)
- For a complete list of events in Vermont, visit https://vermont.com/events/.

Vermont Fall Foliage

Vermont's fall foliage season is one of the most beautiful seasons to visit the state. Visitors come from all over the world to see the brilliant hues of the changing leaves. Depending on the weather, the greatest time to observe fall foliage in Vermont is usually between mid-September to mid-October. Some of Vermont's top sites to see fall foliage include:

- Stowe
- Green Mountain Byway
- Route 100
- Northeast Kingdom
- Lake Champlain Islands
- For more information on Vermont fall foliage, visit https://www.vermontvacation.com/fall/.

Vermont Ski Resorts

Vermont has some of the top ski resorts in the country, with skiing and snowboarding possibilities for all ability levels. Among the most popular ski resorts are:

- Stowe Mountain Resort
- Killington Resort
- Okemo Mountain Resort
- Sugarbush Resort
- Jay Peak Resort
- For more information on Vermont ski resorts, visit https://skivermont.com/.

Vermont Cheese Trail

Vermont is known for its artisanal cheese, and the Vermont Cheese Trail takes you on a tour to meet some of the state's top cheese manufacturers. The trail covers over 40 different cheesemakers, serving cheeses ranging from cheddar to blue cheese. Visit https://www.vtcheese.com/cheese-trail/ for more information about the Vermont Cheese Trail.

Vermont Breweries

Vermont has a booming craft beer culture, with over 60 breweries in the state. Vermont's brewers provide a varied selection of beers that appeal to all tastes, from IPAs to stouts. Among the well-known breweries are:

- The Alchemist Brewery
- Hill Farmstead Brewery
- Lawson's Finest Liquids
- Switchback Brewing Company
- Von Trapp Brewing
- For more information on Vermont breweries, visit https://vermontbrewers.com/.

Vermont Bed and Breakfast Association

Vermont's bed and breakfasts provide a unique and attractive lodging experience, allowing visitors to stay in historic houses and enjoy home-cooked meals. The Vermont Bed and Breakfast Association is an excellent resource for locating the ideal bed and breakfast for your vacation. Visit https://vermontbnbinn.com/ for additional details.

Vermont Farm Tours

A farm tour is a fantastic opportunity to learn about Vermont's agricultural legacy, which is firmly ingrained in the state's culture. Vermont Farm Tours provides a variety of trips that enable tourists to experience Vermont's farms and meet the farmers who make it all possible. They also provide customized trips for groups with specialized hobbies, such as cheese-making or maple sugaring.

Vermont Department of Tourism and Marketing

The website of the Vermont Department of Tourism and Marketing is a comprehensive resource for arranging your visit to the state. It provides information on accommodations, attractions, events, and activities in Vermont. To remain up to speed on the newest events in the state, you can also get a free travel guide or sign up for their e-newsletter.

VermontVacation.com

Another great resource for arranging your vacation to Vermont is VermontVacation.com. It provides information on everything from accommodation to outdoor activities to food options. You may also

~ 183 ~

discover recommended itineraries and travel offers to help you make the most of your visit.

Vermont.org

Vermont.org is the Vermont Chamber of Commerce's official website. It provides information on events, food, shopping, and accommodation around the state. They also have a blog where they provide travel ideas and suggestions for Vermont.

Vermont is a lovely state with enough to offer tourists of all interests. There's something for everyone in this delightful small town, from its spectacular natural beauty to its flourishing food and drink culture.

MAPS OF VERMONT AND BURLINGTON

Maps are a crucial tool for every visitor, whether they are touring a new city or navigating Vermont's country roads. We'll go through the maps that are available for Vermont and Burlington, as well as how to use them to plan your trip.

Vermont is a small state with a lot of natural beauty, beautiful villages, and historic attractions. Whether you're driving, hiking, or bicycling, a decent map can help you make the most of your time here. The Vermont Department of Tourism and Marketing offers a detailed map of the state, complete with highways, important roads, and areas of interest. The map is accessible online and via mail upon request.

The Vermont Atlas and Gazetteer is another handy map for tourists to Vermont. This comprehensive map covers the whole state, from the Green Mountains to Lake Champlain. The Atlas and Gazetteer are especially useful for outdoor enthusiasts since it contains information on hiking paths, campgrounds, and fishing areas. The Atlas and Gazetteer are available for purchase online or through a variety of outdoor merchants.

A city map will help you explore Burlington's various attractions, restaurants, and stores if you want to spend time there. The Burlington Downtown Map offers a comprehensive perspective of the city's downtown region, including Church Street Marketplace, the waterfront, and surrounding neighborhoods. The map is available at many downtown establishments, or you may download a PDF version from the Church Street Marketplace website.

There are several digital maps and applications available to assist you in planning your journey to Vermont. Google Maps is a popular option since it offers thorough instructions as well as real-time traffic information. Vermont's official tourist website also has an interactive map that enables you to explore the state's regions while looking for hotels, restaurants, and activities.

Whichever map you pick, keep in mind that rural portions of Vermont may not have reliable mobile phone coverage. Before you go on your trip, print off a paper copy of your map or download it to your phone.

Consider using a mapping application to generate a custom itinerary while arranging your vacation. You may enter your starting location and destination into websites like Roadtrippers and MapQuest, and the program will build a route that takes your interests and time limits into consideration. These technologies may also assist you in discovering hidden treasures along the journey, such as beautiful views, historic places, and local restaurants.

Visitors visiting Vermont may also get specialist maps. For example, the Vermont Cheese Trail Map highlights the state's many artisanal cheese manufacturers and may be a useful resource for foodies. Another handy map for beer enthusiasts is the Vermont Craft Beer Guide, which features the state's various breweries and brewpubs.

Remember to use the maps and recommendations supplied by local businesses and attractions. Several hotels and bed-and-breakfasts provide maps of the local region, along with food and activity suggestions.

For example, Vermont Farm Tours includes a map of the state's farms as well as a list of tours that enable tourists to meet the farmers and learn about their operations.

A decent map is a crucial tool for every Vermont visitor. A map may help you make the most of your stay in the state, whether you're experiencing the state's natural treasures, attractive small towns, or lively metropolis. There are several alternatives for planning your journey and navigating Vermont's highways, ranging from printed maps to digital applications.

GLOSSARY OF VERMONT TERMS

Vermont is a one-of-a-kind state with distinct cultural and linguistic qualities. These are some popular Vermont terminology and phrases that travelers may come across during their visit:

1. "Maple syrup": Vermont is famous for its maple syrup, which is manufactured from sugar maple sap. Numerous Vermont farms provide tours and samplings of their maple syrup production.

2. "Ski bum": A person who resides in Vermont during the winter months to ski and snowboard.

3. "Creemees": Soft serve ice cream in Vermont. It is a favorite summer dessert and can be found at numerous roadside stalls and ice cream stores.

4. Vermont's moniker, "The Green Mountain State," relates to the state's hilly landscape and lush forests.

5. "Ben & Jerry's": A Vermont-based ice cream business known worldwide for its unusual flavors and dedication to social justice.

6. "The Long Trail" is a 272-mile hiking path that runs from the Massachusetts border to the Canadian border in Vermont.

7. "Phish": A prominent jam band founded in 1983 in Burlington, Vermont.

8. "Flatlander": A person who is not originally from Vermont. It is often used in a pleasant, teasing tone.

9. "The Northeast Kingdom" is an area in Vermont's northeastern portion recognized for its natural beauty and outdoor leisure options.

10. "Sugaring season": The period in late winter and early spring when maple trees are tapped for sap, which is then cooked down to make maple syrup.

11. "Green Up Day": A springtime event in Vermont in which volunteers pick up waste and debris from roadsides and public areas.

12. "Cheese trail": A collection of Vermont cheesemakers and dairy farms, many of which provide tours and sampling of their goods.

13.   "Fall foliage": Vermont is famed for its beautiful autumn foliage when the trees' leaves change to vivid colors of red, orange, and yellow.

14.   "Craft beer": Vermont's craft beer business is growing, with numerous brewers giving tours and sampling their distinctive beers.

15.   "The Mad River Valley" is a picturesque region in central Vermont recognized for its lovely rural villages and outdoor leisure options.

During their visit to Vermont, visitors may come across these and other phrases. Knowing the local language and culture might help tourists enjoy all Vermont has to offer.

CONCLUSION

Vermont is a lovely state that has a lot to offer tourists of all ages and interests. Vermont offers something for everyone, from picturesque drives and outdoor activities to cultural events and delectable local cuisine. Whether you're planning a family vacation, a romantic getaway, or a solo adventure, this guide will help you make the most of your trip.

It is important to consider the best time to visit Vermont while arranging your vacation. Vermont has all four seasons, each with its distinct appeal. The fall foliage season is very popular, but Vermont has lots of outdoor activities throughout the year, including winter, spring, and summer.

Vermont is easily accessible, having many airports and major roads nearby. When you arrive, you must pick where to stay. Vermont has a variety of accommodation options, ranging from luxurious resorts to small bed & breakfasts. Pack accordingly for the season and activities planned, including suitable hiking shoes and warm clothes for milder temps.

Exploring Vermont's natural beauty is one of the highlights of any trip there. Scenic drives are a popular way to enjoy the breathtaking countryside, with choices ranging from the well-known Route 100 to lesser-known back roads. Skiing, hiking, and kayaking are among the many outdoor activities available, all set against the background of the Green Mountains.

Vermont's history is equally rich, and tourists may learn about it by visiting the state's numerous historic sites and museums. Farmers' markets and foodie hotspots give a taste of the local cuisine, while quirky small villages provide a look into Vermont's distinct culture.

Visitors may enjoy cultural events and festivals, top-rated restaurants, and outdoor leisure activities in Burlington, Vermont's biggest city. Day trips and road trip routes nearby provide additional opportunities to see the state's different landscapes and attractions.

Vermont has a variety of family-friendly activities and accommodations. Packing food and entertainment for vehicle journeys is a good idea when traveling with children, as is picking hotels with features like pools and playgrounds.

Vermont prioritizes sustainability, and eco-friendly tourist opportunities abound. Tourists may stay at environmentally friendly hotels and dine at farm-to-table restaurants, while local programs try to safeguard Vermont's ecosystem for future generations.

This book also includes practical information such as travel suggestions, safety guidance, and driving in Vermont. Contacts and websites are useful tools for planning your vacation.

To assist visitors to understand the local culture, the appendix provides maps of Vermont and Burlington, resources, and a dictionary of Vermont terminology.

Vermont is an excellent choice for those seeking a one-of-a-kind and memorable experience. Vermont offers something for everyone, with its natural beauty, rich history, wonderful cuisine, and emphasis on sustainability. Use this guide to plan your ideal vacation and make the most of your time in Vermont

Made in the USA
Las Vegas, NV
04 June 2023

72944419R00115